SECURE

Cultivate Inner Security
with Self-Compassion

Dr. Z. Seda Şahin

To Grandma, Grandpa, Lee, and Lily— thank you for exemplifying the essence of secure relationships. I cherish the memories with all of you and deeply miss you.

&

To my family, friends, mentors, and therapists who stood by me on my journey of self-discovery — thank you for supporting me in cultivating my *Inner Security*. Your encouragement has been invaluable.

&

To my dear clients — I extend heartfelt gratitude for your dedication and resilience, demonstrating that change is not only achievable but also a testament to your unwavering commitment. It is a privilege to accompany you on this transformative journey.

Contents

Prologue

I sat in front of my laptop and waited for my therapist to log on. He'd never been late to any of our sessions over the years, so this felt different. At that moment, I had no idea he was killed the day before.

I waited a little longer and then called him, but he didn't answer. That night, I also sent him an email. I let him know it was okay that he forgot. No worries. It happens. I mean, we'd never had a Saturday session anyway. He's human, too.

Still, no answer. He always answered. He was always there.

On Monday morning, I finally talked to his office manager and received the devastating news: he had been killed in a car accident while riding his bike. It had been fast. He didn't suffer. He died doing what he loved.

I couldn't breathe.

Was I in the plot of a Netflix show? Everything felt so surreal. I had experienced so many losses over the last few years, and grief had become a frequent guest in my life, but I just couldn't accept this loss. It was not the right time. I was not ready.

I suddenly realized that back in graduate school, studying to become a therapist myself, I had never learned how to cope with the sudden death of one's own therapist.

Who do you talk to when your therapist dies?

I don't know. Maybe I'll just talk with you. I guess I'm just trying to make sense of things that don't make sense.

To be honest, I had given up on my dream of publishing this book about cultivating *Inner Security*. I finished it several years ago with the encouragement of my students and clients. My late therapist read it over one weekend and said he loved it because he thought it would help people improve their mental well-being. He also encouraged me to publish it. Shortly after that, COVID-19 hit the world, and I became distracted by everything going on. Being a therapist during a global pandemic wasn't easy, and I didn't have the extra bandwidth for anything else.

So, I let the book go.

After my therapist died, I decided to edit it with my current consciousness and give it another shot. This book is finding you because of him. Maybe this way, I will honor his legacy and pay that valuable support forward. This is for you, Doc. Thank you for everything you did for me. I miss you, and I will be eternally grateful.

Introduction

As a psychotherapist, I have been sharing the skills you will read in this book with my clients for the last two decades. In fact, I've been practicing them myself because therapists are human, and shit happens to us, too! Right off the bat, I wanted to clarify that therapists, well most anyway, are not automatically enlightened beings! Please refer to the prologue for more evidence.

Over the years, I have had the pleasure of witnessing remarkable improvements in my clients' lives following our work together on the concept that I call *Inner Security*. One of my clients on her healing journey recently said:

"I learned to love and accept myself. I now trust myself to make the next right decision for me. I can finally have fun with myself, and no matter what is going on outside, I know I have *Inner Security*. You've offered me a distinct way to approach life, and now I can support myself along the way and welcome the higher intelligence of life."

Inner Security is the deep trust that you can be there for yourself. *Inner Security* is being able to give yourself permission to feel all of your feelings, regardless of what anyone tells you. *Inner Security* means you can see yourself clearly and set life goals according to your core values so you can explore, grow, and contribute.

Cultivating *Inner Security* can be learned and practiced. That is the purpose of this book. Now, I invite you to come on this journey with me and see how you can find the *Inner Security* my clients have learned to experience and enjoy. If you are willing to get out of your comfort zone and be uncomfortable with the unfamiliar, I believe that you will explore many new things about yourself and expand tremendously.

All right then, let's begin our journey! When you are ready, please complete the questionnaire below, with (1) representing 'strongly disagree' and (5) representing 'strongly agree'.

	(1)	(2)	(3)	(4)	(5)
(1) I trust the higher intelligence within me.	○	○	○	○	○
(2) I know myself.	○	○	○	○	○
(3) I am enough.	○	○	○	○	○
(4) I love and accept all parts of me.	○	○	○	○	○
(5) I can take the next step.	○	○	○	○	○
(6) I am worthy of love and support.	○	○	○	○	○
(7) I encourage myself to live life to the fullest.	○	○	○	○	○

	(1)	(2)	(3)	(4)	(5)
(8) I can depend on myself.	○	○	○	○	○
(9) I know that it is okay not to be okay.	○	○	○	○	○
(10) I honor my feelings.	○	○	○	○	○
(11) I am a human being, not a human doing.	○	○	○	○	○
(12) I am open to change.	○	○	○	○	○
(13) I trust my process.	○	○	○	○	○
(14) I can practice self-compassion.	○	○	○	○	○
(15) I like my life.	○	○	○	○	○
(16) I have many strengths.	○	○	○	○	○
(17) I listen to my intuition.	○	○	○	○	○
(18) I love spending time with myself.	○	○	○	○	○

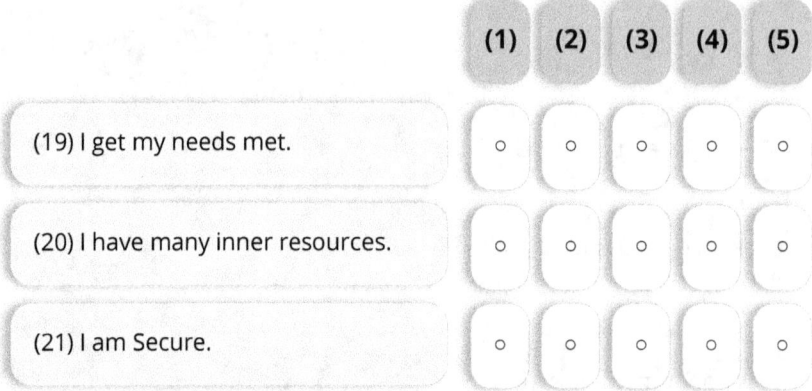

	(1)	(2)	(3)	(4)	(5)
(19) I get my needs met.	○	○	○	○	○
(20) I have many inner resources.	○	○	○	○	○
(21) I am Secure.	○	○	○	○	○

Now, let's dive deeper into how it felt to go through this questionnaire. What thoughts, emotions, and body sensations did you notice as you were completing it? Please take a minute to turn inward and reflect on how this process was for you. Remember, all experiences are welcome here.

You probably saw that there is no answer key to this questionnaire. The external keys that we are searching for outside are actually inside us. By answering these questions, we are just noticing where we fall in the spectrum of living a life with *Inner Security*. After completing the book, you might want to retake this questionnaire and evaluate your growth.

Dear one, I promise that we will go slowly, as creating shifts in our lives may initially be overwhelming. Together, we will travel to a new territory of life with *Inner Security*. But it might be a little bumpy ride, so fasten your seatbelts.

Fair warning: In this book, some sarcasm and even some cussing may be involved. If this book could have a 3D format, there would be many hand gestures in addition to passionate expressions. (What can I say? I'm Mediterranean!) If you are not a fan of either, no hard feelings!

Regarding organization, this book consists of two sections focusing on why we are the way we are and how we can expand who we are. First, we will explore *Inner Security*, one of our most essential resources in life, guiding us toward a fulfilling and peaceful connection with ourselves and others. We will learn about the *Secure Self* and explore what gets in the way of us accessing our *Secure Self*. This path will lead us to welcome different parts of our psyche to have a loving, embracing, and engaging relationship with ourselves.

The exploration of our parts within psychology is not a new concept. It is deeply embedded in the tapestry of psychological theories, reflecting a longstanding acknowledgment that our psyche is multifaceted, comprised of diverse parts or ego states influencing our thoughts and behaviors.

Tracing its roots through therapeutic theories such as Psycho-analytic Therapy, Jungian Therapy, Gestalt Therapy, Transactional Analysis, Psychodrama, and Ego State Therapy, the notion of parts concept has evolved. Recent contributions from approaches like Eye Movement Desensitization and Reprocessing (EMDR) and Internal Family Systems (IFS) have added nuanced layers, enriching this enduring perspective.

Delving into the dynamic landscape of psychological parts, my immersion in Transactional Analysis during the early 2000s became a pivotal exploration. Concurrently, participating in psychodrama group therapy sessions for several years deepened my comprehension and immersed me in profound role-playing explorations of our various, especially wounded, internal parts. As the journey progressed, my doctoral training in systems thinking emerged as a crucial chapter, unveiling the intricate dance of parts within a system. These diverse theoretical frameworks, collaboratively embraced, became the bedrock of my clinical approach—an approach I am eager to share with you.

Going beyond traditional theoretical boundaries, the novel process unveiled in this book intricately weaves Attachment Theory into the core of parts exploration with mindfulness and self-compassion. Rooted in inclusivity and trauma-informed practices, it embraces a perspective of cultural humility, aspiring to guide you on a transformative journey of self-discovery.

In the **second section**, we will create an *Inner Security Toolbox* that will equip you with coping skills that you can use anywhere. You will also learn how to let your *Secure Self* guide your life. Examples of how *Inner Security* can be cultivated and integrated into your daily life with self-compassion will be provided. Together, we will practice creating a *Secure* environment within ourselves so that we can live a more authentic and vibrant life.

Before we take off, let me give you some final details on what to expect on this ride. I will share my professional and personal journey with you during our time together. The client stories I discuss are real and sacred to me. With these experiences, we will recognize the shared humanity of suffering and thriving that we all go through regardless of who we are and where we come from. All client names and identifying information have been changed to maintain confidentiality.

I listened to the wise words of Toni Morrison when she said, "If there's a book that you want to read, but it hasn't been written yet, then you must write it[1]," and I wrote the book I wanted to read. I hope it also meets your needs and provides you with different perspectives. Even if one person finds a remedy in these pages and relates to these experiences, I have done my job as a fellow human being in expanding the universal consciousness.

I must acknowledge that writing a book in a second language is more complicated than I thought, so I apologize in advance for the imperfections in my English. I hope that the original exercises and meditations land well and are helpful. In addition to those practices, I've incorporated research-based information and recommendations as resources for enhancing our resiliency (the comprehensive list of over 125 citations is in the reference section #nerdalert).

I want our journey to be interactive, so throughout the book, I will ask you to look up some things, read, write, and listen. To aid with that, I created a blog to connect with you digitally. You can access the blog posts corresponding to each book chapter at https:// medium.com/@securechapters and find pictures, links, and audio files of the meditations. Together, we will practice what we learn theoretically and experience *Inner Security*.

Having said all that, I need to clarify that this book does **_not_** replace therapy work. My intention is to provide you with resources you might relate to and aim to investigate further. This book is a beginner's guide to exploring our psyche. Trauma processing requires an intimate therapeutic relationship. I encourage you to seek additional professional support if you need a closer ally on your journey.

My last disclaimer concerns the potential side effects of engaging with this work. We can all learn to change, but there are always risks when we do. As we work on our *Inner Security*, the external relationships in our lives may be influenced by this shift. Some people in our circle may perceive this shift as positive, while others may not be as welcoming—especially if the other party might have benefited from you not tending to your needs and boundaries. Be mindful that you might have to let go of some old patterns, people, things, or places to open space for a *Secure* version of you.

And please remember, forming secure bonds within yourself will create more secure relationships with your family, partners, friends, coworkers, neighbors, community, world, and the universe.

This is the power of being *Secure*!

Section 1

Inner Security

CHAPTER 1

———— ❧ ————

Secure Self

Mother Nature draws a fantastic painting on the beach in Uvita, Costa Rica, only at certain times of the day. During low tide, the beach undergoes a natural transformation, creating an extension of sand and rocks that remarkably resemble a whale's tail. You can walk until the end of the tail, depending on the tide, and look at this beautiful land from the ocean's perspective. Later on, as the ocean gradually rises, the two parts of the beach disappear and become one. The powerful ocean completely takes over, and the parts are whole again. Every day, you can observe this natural dance and marvel at the gravitational forces of the universe.

We also inevitably form different parts of our psyche when strong forces pull us. These parts help us to survive in life, but now we miss out on being the ocean. Unfortunately, most of us eventually forget that we are this powerful ocean of consciousness called the *Secure Self*. This book will guide you on the journey back to this wholeness.

Dear one, we are all born *Secure*. Each and every one of us. We are miracle beings coming into this world to explore what it means to be human for a short time. Just look at the incredible inner workings of our body and the trillions of cells working intricately without us doing anything. Not only is there this unique internal architecture, but the genius beauty of the universe is also right in front of us. Our galaxy, which has about 400 billion stars, is only one of the two trillion galaxies in the universe[1]. Lucky does not even begin to describe our chances to exist in this marvelous space.

Fun fact (please insert Dr. Sheldon Cooper's voice to read this paragraph): In 1957, trailblazer astrophysicist E. Margaret Burbidge and her colleagues published an article called "Synthesis of the Elements in Stars" about how all the elements in our world come from the thermonuclear reactions of the stars[2]. Starting with hydrogen and helium as the universe's only elements, billions of years later, other elements started forming from further star explosions.

So, yes, it is true; we are all made of stars. If we zoom into the cells in our bodies, we will find the same oxygen, carbon, and calcium atoms that were once in the core of a star. This means we are all from the same source and part of this interconnected web of consciousness that we have yet to understand. Now, isn't that fantastic?

Our *Secure Self* is our direct connection portal to the rest of this amazing universe. This abundant consciousness knows that we have part of the cosmos within us and reminds us that we are part of something bigger than ourselves and we are all connected.

Being *Secure* doesn't mean we are perfect. Being *Secure* means loving and accepting who we are as we are. When we let the *Secure Self* be in the driver's seat of our lives, there is trust and ease. We are confident in who we are, and also, just like the rest of the universe, we are dedicated to expanding our consciousness. We have many capabilities and resources. We trust the higher intelligence within us and can make decisions with that guidance. We are eager to learn and grow. We feel the zest of life and the universe's flow.

From the day that we are born, our *Secure Self* guides us to find our truths, values, and callings. If we listen closely, we will hear our *Secure Self's* voice telling us: "Darling, your essence is love. You are enough. You are loved. You are worthy. You are *Secure*. You already know what you need in this life; now, go for it."

You might also call the *Secure Self,* the divine self, the true self, the Self, the authentic self, the higher self, higher consciousness, or [insert your spiritual figure]-like self, depending on your preference. Different cultures, religions, psychological theories, and philosophies discuss the self. Each approach is like one of the crystal pieces of a beautiful chandelier. Each piece reflects a different interpretation of the source, but only one source exists.

At the beginning of our incredible life journey, we love ourselves unconditionally. As babies, we don't look at ourselves in the mirror, worry, and say things like, "Oh my goodness, look at this muffin top. Geez, I need to hit the gym. I have to get so much done today. I shouldn't be feeling this way. What is wrong with me? Am I ok? Am I enough?"

When we first come to this world from this abundant source, we do not have the learned destructive thoughts and behaviors like racism, sexism, homophobia, xenophobia, ableism, ageism, or any other discriminatory behavior towards ourselves or others. These all come after we are exposed to different cultural messages and experiences. Slowly but surely, we become conditioned to respond similarly from the box we identify with and don't even wonder what else is out there.

Unfortunately, over time, we tend to lose connection with our *Secure Self* because life happens. And it happens to all of us. Then, the other parts, the Anxious and Avoidant Parts, start emerging as coping mechanisms. These parts, which we will explore soon, slowly expand and might take over until we pause and are willing to look at our core, our *Secure Self.* This is the work we will be doing together.

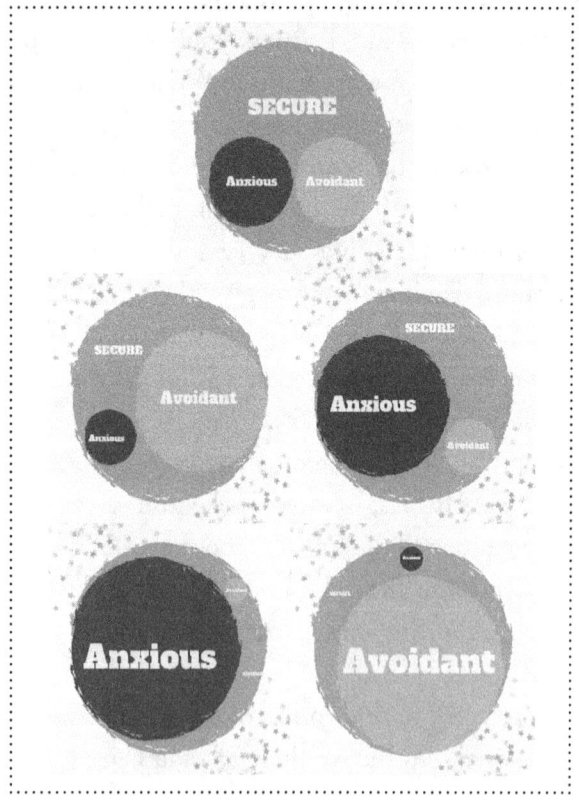

The *Secure Self's* erosion eventually leads to the Anxious and Avoidant Parts taking more and more charge of our lives. The dominance of these parts depends on our life experiences and the transgenerational transmissions of patterns. Therefore, for some of us, the *Secure Self* can remain more prominent than other parts, while some develop substantial Anxious and Avoidant Parts.

The different patterns of these parts create humankind's incredible diversity, which is worthy of celebration. This fantastic mosaic inside each and every one of us is like our fingerprint: unique and special. Each part is essential for our survival and serves a purpose. It is now our responsibility to explore the intention of these parts and let our *Secure Self* take the driver's seat of our lives so we can enjoy *Inner Security*. A beautiful journey is waiting for us.

It is my pleasure to guide others to access their *Secure Self* and ride alongside them on their voyage of discovery. I still remember a participant from a workshop I conducted at a conference in Indiana in 2019. When she came to talk to me after the presentation, she shared about the shame she previously felt because of not having a secure attachment style due to her adverse childhood experiences.

She then shared how she was pleasantly surprised to hear this new perspective, which has brought her hope and motivation. She said she never realized that she had a *Secure Self*, nor did she expect to meet her *Secure Self* during one of the meditations. Her honesty and vulnerability touched me very much. I thanked her for her courage and appreciated this gift she had given me.

You and I, together, will practice accessing this *Secure Self*, which is always present and waiting for us to follow its lead. When my *Secure Self* guides me—even during my childhood—I feel incredible joy and connection to everything and everyone around me. I am in the flow. I feel supported by life. I trust the intelligence within me.

I feel whole. I feel *Secure*. It is such a lovely and peaceful place to be, and I wish I could stay here more often.

Okay, moving on from sounding like a hippie on LSD from the 60s (I know some of you were just thinking that!) to sounding more like an academic (I apologize!), I thought I should turn to research to explore how we can access the *Secure Self* more often. As an investigative researcher, I was especially interested in finding specific ways to cultivate *Inner Security* so that I could help my clients more efficiently.

Of course, the research area I turned to was the original attachment theory, which is based on the work of Dr. John Bowlby and Dr. Mary Ainsworth, that I've been fond of (Umm, maybe a tad more than fond of since that's what I mainly did my doctoral dissertation on, and I loved it.).

Unfortunately, my attachment theory research led me to find questionnaires only about attachment security in our relationships with our caregivers, partners, friends, or other essential attachment figures. In all of these studies, the attachment security measured was about the external relationships, creating a challenge when we want to understand the quality of the internal relationship that we have with ourselves. (Wait, what? Nooooo!!!!! This cannot be true! Houston, we have a problem[3]!)

Then, I stopped and asked myself, "Why don't *I* create a questionnaire to explore how we relate to ourselves and identify ways to cultivate *Inner Security*?" Now, I have to admit that I doubted myself for a bit. "Can I do this?" I questioned myself. I wasn't an old white cisgender man, so could *I* really contribute to the field of psychology? (Please insert a sarcastic eye roll here.)

After letting go of all the entirely bullshit and socially constructed doubtful thoughts from my mind, I realized I was intrigued by how our inner dialogues would sound if we let our *Secure Self* be our guide and experienced *Inner Security*. The introductory questionnaire you've completed emerged through this exploration. This process helped me identify specific steps to remember and reconnect with our *Secure Self*—steps we'll actively engage in the upcoming chapters.

Additionally, I was curious to see how our internal conversations changed, depending on which part of our psyche was more in charge. This investigation led me to construct the parts questionnaires you will access in the following chapters.

With my wish to create a roadmap to help others (and myself) ease the pain of being human and find ways to thrive, I wanted to delve into exploring how we can effectively and compassionately support ourselves and constructively relate to our different parts.

In the beginning, the complexity of our inner architecture overwhelmed me. However, after spending thousands of hours with my clients, I have seen many commonalities that we all experience, regardless of where we come from. Considering that 99.6 percent of our genes are identical[4], this made total sense to me. I hope this roadmap will guide you in rediscovering your *Secure Self* and experience *Inner Security*.

Welcome to this journey!

CHAPTER 2

—◦∞◦—

Getting to Know Ourselves

I had tears of gratitude and a sweet tenderness in my heart when I stood before Rumi's tomb in Konya, Türkiye, on a hot summer day in 2015. It was my first time there, and I found myself to be very emotional. This spiritual teacher's words have helped me immensely in my dark moments and given me the light I needed to be able to take the following steps, so it was a privilege to be there.

While walking on the grounds where Rumi taught 800 years ago, I remembered one of my favorite pieces from him called "The Guest House[1]." In his famous poem, Rumi encourages us to welcome all of our emotions as visitors. He asks us to consider them guests with important messages for us to hear and honor. He gently connects us to something bigger than us by reminding us of our limited understanding of life as human beings. He wants us to consider that the reason for these visits might be above and beyond our current consciousness level.

Wouldn't inviting these messengers and listening to what they are trying to say be helpful? I know this might not be easy, especially when challenging emotions are visiting us and not planning to leave for a while. Truthfully, I am not a big fan of these unexpected, annoying visitors either (sorry, Rumi!). I don't really like feeling these uncomfortable emotions, and I don't want them to stay long.

It is usually hard to make sense of these unexpected visits when we are in the thick of it. Let's be honest; we usually can't wait for them to be done and gone, right? But maybe, as Rumi says, their purpose is beyond our understanding at the moment. And perhaps our future self will smile and be grateful for these visitors delivering critical information. Maybe, we will eventually see the big picture and thank them for their visits. Are you open to this possibility?

This approach is a loving, embracing, and engaging response to our emotions. We can learn this new way of relating to ourselves and utilize our fantastic internal guidance system. Instead of trying to get rid of our feelings or being completely overridden by them, we can work on changing our relationship with them.

This may seem complicated, but there is a small first step that we can take to begin this process. We can start by sitting with ourselves quietly and being attuned to our inner experiences. We can get to know ourselves from this welcoming place and practice showing love and respect to all parts of ourselves.

I don't know about you, but the beginning phase of learning how to sit with my messy mind was like torture. I had the chance to attend silent meditation retreats in the pre-pandemic era, where I started becoming familiar with my thoughts and feelings. These retreats allowed me to work on my *Inner Security* by spending quality time with myself in a safe space where I could freely feel shitty. (Apparently, feeling shitty is part of life! Who knew!)

I learned to sit with my emotions without judgment until they moved through me. My teachers were very helpful in creating this container where we could compassionately and safely hold anything that arose in the process. But to be honest, my first couple of silent retreats were pretty tough. My mind was racing at 250 miles per hour, and I didn't know how to deal with that. I remember sitting on my cushion as waves of thoughts hit me.

"This cushion hurts. My back hurts. Why is my sock itching? Oh, my goodness, my stomach is making so much noise. I wonder what's for lunch. That spinach quiche yesterday was so good. Am I the worst meditator in this room? Wait, will someone grade us? How long are we going to sit like this? Exactly what am I supposed to do with my breath now? What does 'focusing on my breath' even mean? That's weird. Who focuses on their breath? What is there in my breath to focus on? Is it because English is my second language that I don't get this? May I get a translator, please? I wonder what's for lunch; I'm getting hungry. Ok, I should go back to my breath. I wonder if my breath stinks. Did I brush my teeth after breakfast? I think I did, but I had tea after brushing my teeth. Maybe I should have had a snack with that tea. Oh, geez, how many more minutes? Why doesn't someone ring the bell already? Wait, what? That was only the first two minutes of the sitting. Oh shit!"

I want to set the record straight. Going to these silent meditation retreats doesn't mean you'll reach Nirvana. I don't know about other participants, but I am nowhere near enlightened. In those weeks, I hated not having the distractions of our daily lives. No talking, no texting, no books, no social media, and no Netflix for a WHOLE week. It does sound like torture, doesn't it?

In the beginning, I would agree with that conclusion. It was as if I was addicted to these distractions, and I was struggling with detoxing from all of them. At those moments, I bet my wise and loving meditation teachers, Rebecca and Candace, were happy that I even showed up. (I just know that after the silent sittings, they returned to their room and said, "Yay, she got up in the morning and came to the meditation hall," while high-fiving each other with their happy dance. Okay, they might not have done any of these things, but I saw it in their eyes. I really did!)

The mud started settling down as I continued to sit and spend time with my mind and body. I slowly began to see myself more clearly. The more I accepted my experience, myself, and my needs compassionately, the more my heart opened. This made me more tolerant of staying with my experiences, regardless of their discomfort. I gradually developed more bandwidth and finally started experiencing *Inner Security*.

Ok, enough with the talk. Let's practice turning inward and start spending some quality time with ourselves. The audio recording of the meditation can be accessed on the blog in the *Chapter 2* post (https://medium.com/@securechapters). Would you like to join me?

Meditation Practice

For those who wish to become more familiar with meditation, I want to reassure you that if you can breathe, you can meditate. I'm not promising you'll like it, but I'm sure you can do it.

Please take a seat somewhere you can sit comfortably, or feel free to lie down if you prefer. Either close your eyes or turn your gaze downwards—the point is to feel comfortable and safe in this position. You will be charging your mind's battery for the next few minutes.

Also, please make sure your phones are silenced so there is a short period that you are not distracted. This will prove that the world will continue spinning if we're not on our phones for a few minutes.

Let's all start by focusing on our breath. Find the place in your body where you feel your breath the most. This is going to be your anchor. This can be your nose, the chest area, the diaphragm, or the abdomen. We will bring our attention to our anchor when we feel lost or distracted. For now, just remember that.

Now, focus on what happens in your body when you slowly inhale. Next, focus on what happens when you slowly exhale. Follow the breath as it enters your body, travels in your body, and exits your body. Inhale and exhale. Inhale and exhale.

Just continue this practice for a few more minutes. Inhaling and exhaling. Inhaling and exhaling.

And meanwhile, your mind will inevitably wander about what you have to do as you sit and breathe. The dishes waiting for you or the email you have not responded to might come to your mind. Or random questions may arise: "Did I write that doctor's appointment on my calendar? What will I be making for dinner? What exactly is the purpose of this exercise?" These are all okay and normal.

Inhaling and exhaling... Inhaling and exhaling...

Whether you have meditated for 10,000 hours or if this is your first time, those thoughts, feelings, body sensations, and many other distractions will always knock on your mind's door. The key is just to keep breathing.

When this happens, gently return your attention to your breath as that anchor. You might even say thank you to the distractions if you'd like. Just continue noticing your breath when you get distracted for a few more seconds. I'm right here with you.

Inhale, exhale and be proud of yourself for giving yourself these few minutes of breathing—of simply being—as a beautiful gift. Inhale and exhale.

And when you are ready, slowly open your eyes. Make sure to congratulate yourself for spending quality time with your thoughts and practicing a new skill.

How was that experience for you? Whether this is something you've been practicing for a while or it was your first time, thank you for trying. Mindfulness meditation builds the muscle of returning to our breath, which helps us come back to the present moment. Especially when we are watching the movies of the past or the future in our minds, this will be valuable for us to return to the here and now. This is the practice of fully engaging with the present instead of trying to change or avoid what it is, and it is an essential skill of allowing life to *be* instead of trying to control it.

Notice how you felt throughout this practice. For some, it may be relaxing; for others, it may feel unpleasant and all in between. Even though meditation might not be something everyone enjoys, it is something everyone can practice. We can think about it like a muscle we are building in our mind's gym.

We now have decades of scientific evidence about how meditation is beneficial for our mental and physical health, such as increasing the gray matter[2] in our brain to help us better manage anxiety and depression[3,4]. Meditation promotes better sleep[5], weight regulation[6,] a more robust immune system[7], increased attention[8], and job performance[9].

In 2017, the first epigenetic research findings showed that long-term meditation slows the aging process[10] (could this be why I look younger than my age?). And do you know what the best thing in all of this is? It's free!

For meditation to be effective, just like any other practice, it needs to become habitual. Our self-awareness becomes more precise as we sit with who we are more often and become friends with ourselves.

But how do we become friends with someone? How do we get to know them? How do we learn what they like and what they don't like? How do we pick up on how to support them?

Though there may be many different answers, the most common responses I've received when I asked my clients these questions were to spend quality time and to be curious. Then, why wouldn't we do that to get to know ourselves? If we want to become our own ally, friend, supporter, coach, or motivator, we need to know ourselves from the inside out. And spending 10-15 minutes a day practicing this leads the way.

The more we show up for ourselves and realize that we can be with all these different experiences, thoughts, emotions, body sensations, and even the Oscar-worthy catastrophic movies we shoot in our minds when stressed, the more we cultivate *Inner Security*.

Through these practices, eventually, we will notice that the distance between our innermost experiences and our *Secure Self* expands. Slowly but surely, we will start becoming the wholeness of this consciousness and experience *Inner Security*.

CHAPTER 3

———— ✲ ————

Am I Doomed?

When I visited Medellin, Colombia, I was in awe of this city's incredible resiliency. How did the murder capital of the world turn its destiny around to become the most innovative city in the world? I wondered. Listening to the ins and outs of where the city was, and the steps it took to re-create itself gave me so much hope. I also felt so fortunate to learn about this transformation during my healing journey—such a synchronicity.

Like Medellin, most of us have experienced challenging events in some way, shape, or form. We get knocked down and sometimes struggle to get up. Unfortunately, these experiences take a toll on us and influence how we relate to ourselves and the world around us. Does that mean we're all doomed?

Nope, we definitely are not. The good news is that the research over the last forty years tells us we can change. Our brains do not stop growing, shifting, and expanding. Our brains are not fixed; they can transform and generate new neural pathways.

This fantastic brain flexibility is also true for other living beings. For instance, canaries have particular neurons in their brains related explicitly to communicating through singing, which increases in size as the season changes[1]. If the canaries can do it, we can do it!

Unfortunately, due to the pressures of life, we often forget how resilient we are. When I was talking to a friend of mine who was a taxi driver in my hometown of Izmir, Türkiye, he told me about some challenges he was facing and was unsure if he could change himself enough to make different decisions. Obviously, that felt like the perfect time for me to tell him about one specific study of the brain structures of taxi drivers in London (I know, I know! I can't help it! #nerdalert).

Researchers found that the section in the taxi drivers' brains responsible for directions, their hippocampi, was much more developed than in people who didn't spend as much time driving[2]. This was only one example of how the brain has the power to transform depending on what we choose to practice.

After sharing that insight with my friend, his face lit up, and he was suddenly very proud of what his brain could do. He also became hopeful about creating new changes in his brain if he put his mind to it. My work was done!

If you were wondering if researchers came up with a fancy word for this phenomenon (yes, you are right, of course, they did!), it is called **neuroplasticity**[3]. This means the brain is flexible and, depending on which skills you learn and practice, can create more connections in that area of your brain. Neuropsychologist Donald Hebb said it best: The neurons that fire together wire together[4]. So, which new neurons do you want to wire in your brain?

At the beginning of the 1990s, his holiness the Dalai Lama kindly challenged Dr. Richard Davidson, an internationally renowned researcher on the brain and emotions, to study resilience, happiness, and compassion in his lab[5]. In the years that followed, Buddhist monks helped to advance science and shared their brain scans with the rest of the world.

These monks had at least 10,000 hours of meditation experience. Their brain scans allowed Dr. Davidson and his team to show results similar to those of the taxi driver study. They scientifically proved that meditation alters brain structure and function[6]. Their article "Buddha's Brain: Neuroplasticity and Meditation" identified that these changes range "from the growth of new connections to the creation of new neurons"[7]. Isn't that pretty amazing?

When we examine how our brains adapt to surviving threats, we see that evolution has wired us all in a specific way to adjust to living in stressful situations. We are all biologically constructed to pay more attention to what can go wrong to stay alive. This is called the *negativity bias[8]*, which was a great strategy when humans were in the wild and trying not to be eaten by different predators. However, it may not be as useful in our current stage of evolution.

After thousands of years of practicing the negativity bias, we arrive at the current day. When life, in addition to personal adversities, adds a pandemic, economic uncertainty, and wars into the mix, it makes sense why our overworked nervous system will keep us alert, especially waking us up at 3 am trying to solve all the problems in our lives.

What is Happening in Our Brains?

Let's explore what takes place in our brains as we receive constant information from our environments. Our autonomic nervous system

(ANS), responsible for involuntary responses such as heart rate, re-spiratory rate, and blood pressure, has three parts: the sympathetic, the parasympathetic, and the enteric nervous systems[9].

Our sympathetic nervous system (fight/flight/freeze/fawn re-sponse) gets activated when our brains perceive a threat in the envi-ronment. In contrast, our parasympathetic nervous system (rest and digest response) is turned on when we feel relaxed and grounded[9]. Lastly, the gastrointestinal functions, through "a network of neu-rons and glia," are regulated by independently functioning enteric nervous system[10].

During times of perceived danger, our brain's emotion center, the limbic system, becomes highly active and takes over our cognitive processes. This is because the amygdala, an almond-shaped structure within the limbic system, gets triggered and overrides the rest of our brain. As a result, we lose access to the pre-frontal cortex, which is responsible for critical thinking, perspective-taking, and other executive functions. The world-renowned trauma expert Dr. Bessel van der Kolk calls the amygdala our "smoke detector"[11]. Our amygdala does a fantastic job of scanning our surroundings and ringing the alarm bells when it senses potential threats.

This evaluation process is mostly unconscious, which means that any perceived danger can trigger an immediate response from our sympathetic nervous system. However, until we become aware of these potential threats, this screening will continue to operate in the background, trying to keep us safe without us even realizing it.

Neuroplasticity creates new train tracks in our brains instead of automatically continuing a sympathetic nervous system response. Research has shown that long-term meditators have less activation in their amygdala than novice meditators, proving that our brain can be transformed[6].

In the upcoming chapters, you will learn about how various parts of our psyche are developed due to the consistent activation of the sympathetic nervous system; in other words, when life happens. You will also discover specific techniques to activate your parasympathetic nervous system, which can lead to enhanced well-being and a greater sense of calm. Ultimately, by befriending our nervous system, we can become more self-regulated, resilient, and better equipped to handle whatever life throws our way.

Now, since we have already established that change is possible (thanks to neuroplasticity) but not easy (thanks to negativity bias), we need to look at how to cultivate compassion and wisdom for a sustainable transformation (just like Medellin) from a nervous system informed perspective. This will be the gateway to generating a more secure relationship with ourselves.

The Speech

The process of changing the way we relate to ourselves and cultivating *Inner Security* has always piqued my interest. In 2015, I began discussing practical methods for transforming our inner dialogues using the Gestalt empty chair technique to create a more *Secure* environment within ourselves. This was the first time I took a risky step by being completely honest, talking about the voices in my head with the public, and fearing that I would be misunderstood. But I took a deep breath and started anyway.

Welcome everyone,

How many of you want to be better speakers? How many of you want to be better at your job? How many of you want to be better partners or better parents?

In that space where we are and where we want to be lies the biggest challenge of our lives. An internal struggle that all of us experience. Whether this is a professional or a personal discrepancy, it might end up leaving us feeling defeated and not enough.

The voices in our heads when we feel "not enough" might deliver conflicting messages, which might cause even more suffering.

Let's take a look at our real-life challenges.

How many of you have given a speech where you needed to remember a part and stumbled? I have.

How many of you have made a mistake at work? I have.

How many of you, when you were in an argument, said things to your partner that you later came to regret? Oh my gosh, bless my poor partner.

How many of you felt inadequate as a parent and wished there was a handbook for raising kids?

We have all been there, even though we might feel that we are one of the few selected unlucky ones. And when this happens, a debate starts in our minds with powerful voices. In my mind, there are three dominant voices. I don't know about you, but it can get pretty noisy up there.

Of course, first, the critical voice takes action (I sit in one of the three chairs on the stage). Here's what mine often sounds like:

How could you do that, Seda? What on earth were you thinking? I just cannot believe how stupid that was. You should have definitely thought about that before.

When we hear these, then the other part of us, our Inner Child, starts shrinking and feeling inadequate, not enough (I switch chairs and go to the second one). Mine says: I'm not enough. I'm not smart enough, I'm not strong enough, I'm not good enough.

And the speed of this interaction is so fast that most of us aren't even aware of the process. We end up feeling frustrated with ourselves and may even become irritable. And you know who gets the experience of this grouchiness? Our loved ones.

I want to talk about one way of overcoming this internal struggle. It starts with awareness about what's going on inside of us. Because without awareness, we are going to repeat the same habitual thoughts and behaviors. Awareness opens the door to change. As Victor Frankl says, it is in the space between stimulus and response where the choices lie12. When we can raise awareness, we can choose whom to listen to.

Yes, there is another option to which we can listen. Another radio station plays a different tape with a more compassionate and kinder voice. Just the one we are used to hearing from our support systems when we call them when we're feeling down.

That voice might say: (I sit in the third chair)

You know what, Seda, you've tried really hard, and you have gotten so much better than you could have thought at the beginning of all this. You are more confident and capable, and I'm proud of you. Even if things didn't go exactly as you had hoped, it is still pretty amazing, and I'm confident you will keep getting better and better. Seda, your goal isn't perfection. It is to keep trying and learning, and you are wonderful at doing that. I trust you and your perseverance.

(I get up and walk to the front of the stage)

I don't know about you, but I need to listen to that voice (pointing to the third chair). I also want to underline that this debate is normal. It was comforting to me to realize it is part of the human condition to have these debates. Everybody has these debates in their minds to different degrees. Actually, the only people who do not have this debate are psychopaths because they have no critical voice; they lack empathy and guilt.

So now, it is time to silence that "obnoxious, critical, know-it-all, I'll manage your life" voice.

It's time to give a reality check to the "I'm not enough" voice.

And it is time to record and listen to a more compassionate and kinder voice.

It's a choice.

At that moment, I felt utterly vulnerable. I was already fed up with pretentious interactions and speeches. I valued authenticity and vulnerability; enough was enough. So, I returned to my seat feeling proud and relieved (ok, I have to admit that I had just listened to Brené Brown's talk about vulnerability for the billionth time and may or may not have been influenced by that! If you'd also like some inspiration, you can watch this TED talk by searching for the title "The Power of Vulnerability[13]." By the way, can someone from Microsoft correct the Word program so that when I write 'Brené,' it doesn't have a red mark below it? I mean, how dare Word try to fix her great name! Bill, come on, geez!).

The response from the audience to my utterly transparent speech was entirely unexpected for me. Multiple people approached me afterward and shared how much they related to my experiences. One even asked me how I could read their mind, as they always assumed they were the only ones having these thoughts. This was one of the most touching moments of my life, realizing we are not alone in our human experience; we all struggle with these inner voices, and we often fall into similar dark holes.

———∞———

CHAPTER 4

From Hole to Whole

AUTOBIOGRAPHY IN FIVE SHORT CHAPTERS

- by Portia Nelson

Chapter One

I walk down the street.
There is a deep hole in the sidewalk.
I fall in.
I am lost… I am helpless.
It isn't my fault.
It takes forever to find a way out.

Chapter Two

I walk down the same street.
There is a deep hole in the sidewalk.

I pretend I don't see it.
I fall in again.
I can't believe I am in the same place.
But it isn't my fault.
It still takes a long time to get out.

Chapter Three

I walk down the same street.
There is a deep hole in the sidewalk.
I see it is there.
I still fall in… it's a habit.
My eyes are open.
I know where I am.
It is my fault… I get out immediately.

Chapter Four

I walk down the same street.
There is a deep hole in the sidewalk.
I walk around it.

Chapter Five

I walk down another street.

You are not alone, dear one. Many of us are looking for something that will fulfill us—that degree, that job, that partner, that child, that bank account, that house, that car, that trip, that many followers, and the list goes on. But, even if we get this external stuff, most of us still live with that hole we don't know how to fill. And when the emptiness hits, the arbitrary search to fill it starts again and again. We chase the carrot with these moving targets, day in and out, trying to compensate with different things. Inevitably, we keep falling back into this hole. So, the question we're really after is this: *How do we get from hole to whole?*

When I started my inner healing journey, my therapist shared Portia Nelson's poem[1] with me, which normalized my ups and downs and helped me not to give up. The outline of what we will be doing in this book couldn't be laid out better than these chapters, so I wanted to share this roadmap with you as we embark on our journey together.

We all want the solutions immediately (I do, too!). However, examining what may happen on the way can be the light we need in the dark. When we understand the why, it will be easier to get to how. These chapters, which have stayed with me all these years, can remind us that when we keep walking, continue doing our inner work, and carry the intention to heal, our *Secure Self* will guide us to the next chapter of our journey.

Chapter One

Have you ever been in a situation where you had a visceral reaction of disbelief and shock? Maybe you've gotten some unexpected terrible news; maybe you just realized something hurtful, or maybe even when you tried your hardest, your life didn't go according to your plans. Maybe you experienced a trauma that impacted you profoundly. Or maybe there is a pattern in your life that you keep repeating even though you know that it is destructive for you. That is our **Chapter One**.

If you ever find yourself here, it's okay, dear one. There's nothing wrong with you for being in this darkness. We all fall into this hole from time to time. Traumas and challenging life experiences are inevitable. This is part of being human and living on this weird thing called planet Earth. So, it's okay to get lost and take a break. It's okay not to know which direction to go. It's okay not to have the answers yet. It's okay not to have enough energy to change. It's okay to feel stuck. It's okay to feel what you are exactly feeling.

So many chain reactions had to happen for you to be in this exact place you are in your life. Hundreds of your ancestors had to make certain decisions for you to exist, and many other causes and conditions got you where you are. Being exactly where we are is not our fault, but it is our responsibility to learn how to climb up and get out of the hole.

I must warn you here; unfortunately, the first few chapters of this journey can be pretty lonely. This is where the darkness is so thick, and we do not yet have enough *Inner Security* tools to get out quickly. We know we are in the hole, but we need clarification about why we are in it and, more importantly, what will get us out. We might feel disconnected from others at this stage. We might think we are the only ones in the dark; no one else knows how this darkness feels. Whatever you are experiencing, dear one, many others in different parts of the world feel like you. You are not alone. We are all trying to figure life out and sometimes falling into this hole miserably.

Would you please put your hand on your heart and repeat with me:

"May I begin to let my *Secure Self* be my guide."
May I love and accept myself with all my parts.
May I be gentle with myself in this learning process.
May I feel the power of others traveling on this life journey with me.

Thank you, dear one. Thank you for your bravery and vulnerability. It takes courage to look at the holes in our lives. I just wanted to share how impressed I am that you are taking the leap of faith to live a more authentic and vibrant life. It is my honor to walk alongside you.

Chapter Two

As we continue this journey, we will explore and get to know ourselves more deeply. We will practice sitting and spending time with ourselves. We will begin to examine why the challenges we experience may keep repeating themselves. In different places and at different times, we might find ourselves dealing with the same problems over and over: similar partners, similar friends, similar bosses, and similar relationships.

Yes, I know it is hard to accept that this is the same shitty street and the same shitty hole. Initially, this introspection might sting a bit, but we can tolerate the short-term discomfort for the long-term benefit of living with honesty and clarity.

The person struggling between the person we were and the person we will be needs a lot of emotional support. Thus, we will be providing compassion to ourselves for choosing the same street and falling into the same hole as if we were supporting a dear friend.

A little bit of caution here: realizing these truths might bring up shame, which can be overwhelming (I've been there!). We might think there is something wrong with us. Therefore, we will use the guidance of Rumi to welcome all our emotions and wounded parts. We will listen to and honor their messages.

Chapter Three

We will inevitably find ourselves on the same street again and again. This can be very frustrating now that we know what we are doing, but we cannot stop doing it immediately. Dear one, the neural pathways in our brains for this way of living are very well-traveled, so let's not judge ourselves harshly, okay?

Taking a detour from this highway and deciding to go on this different, untraveled path can be accomplished with knowledge and courage. Our brains will tend to choose familiarity over uncertainty, even if the unfamiliar might be better for us. Therefore, until the unknown becomes familiar, we will be patient with ourselves.

In this chapter, we will take responsibility for our future as we make peace with our past. We will make decisions different from our old programming and risk creating something new from the unknown. We will begin to pave this new path in our brains with the tools we will build together and practice being a secure base and a safe haven for ourselves. This new neural pathway will need to be traveled many times to become the preferred one, so this process will take time and repetition. We will provide this well-deserved patience and love to ourselves.

Chapter Four

Even though we find ourselves entering the same street, we will see the hole and not fall into it this time in **Chapter Four**. We will not repeat the pattern that took us down. This will be the beginning of our new life. How exciting!

With the practiced self-compassion and self-love, we will change our relationship with the hole. We will understand why it is there, show kindness to ourselves, and then walk around it with the guidance of our *Secure Self*.

Here, the yearning for more from our lives than our pasts will surface. The seeds of transformation that we have been planting will eagerly want to blossom. We will want to travel to different streets, to go out and explore the world. We will want to feel the aliveness and be in the flow. We will want to be *Secure*.

This is the transitional phase where there might still be some struggle as we shed the old self. A gentle reminder: Change is not linear, and we might slip up; thus, let's give ourselves some grace and sit with the knowledge that this is part of the transformation process. Dear one, this process can be excruciating, but it is necessary for us to go back to being whole.

Chapter Five

Finally, our *Secure Self* will direct us to a completely different street in **Chapter Five**. This will be a more scenic and interesting road, and we will feel proud of ourselves for being able to choose this new one. Things will be smoother here because our boundaries will keep us safer. We will express our needs and feel more competent in handling life's challenges. We will regulate ourselves more efficiently and make decisions according to our values in life.

There will be much more energy when our body, mind, and heart are aligned. With this energy, we will use our authentic voice and connect with ourselves and others. We will celebrate who we are and be happy to get to know other kindred spirits along the way.

Traveling in this new street will be so much more exciting. We will receive the guidance as inspirations, coincidences, serendipities, or, as I call it, "downloads from the universe." We will feel that we are in the flow often, and there will be ease in our lives. The way we relate to ourselves and others will be kinder, and we won't take life so seriously.

We will laugh more, and we will feel deeply. We will focus on what we can influence and finally give up the illusion of control. We will feel the peace from surrendering to life's order. Eventually, we will realize that we have gained valuable wisdom on our path and use this growth to transform our lives and others.

The Growth After Getting Out of the Hole

The first time I heard about the concept of post-traumatic growth was at a workshop in the fall of 2002 when I was attending the Turkish Psychological Association's annual conference in Ankara, Türkiye. I was in my senior year of college studying psychology and was ready to take on the world. I was familiar with post-traumatic stress but had never heard of post-traumatic growth. I was very curious (#nerdalert).

In the workshop, Dr. Richard Tedeschi introduced this new concept he and Dr. Lawrence Calhoun coined at the University of North Carolina at Charlotte several years back. Their research has confirmed that after traumatic events, individuals can create new possibilities in life, find personal strength, appreciate life, observe shifts in relationships with others, and experience spiritual changes[2].

These individuals also experience living life more deeply and savoring the moments of joy. They relate to themselves and others more authentically. They stop tolerating toxic behaviors in others and can draw more precise boundaries. They often have spiritual awakenings and feel connected to a force bigger than themselves. They become mentally stronger and tolerate uncertainty better.

All I can say is that this presentation was so compelling that it impacted my personal and professional life trajectory. I was so impressed with this holistic way of examining what it looks like to be in chapter five.

Dr. Tedeschi shared their recent research about the post-traumatic growth of resilient New Yorkers after the horrific tragedy of the 9/11 terrorist attack that happened the year before. He showed us a video of these personal transformations, and we all were so touched. He told us that the American Psychological Association would release this video in the USA on the same day, and we were the first privileged ones to watch it due to the time difference. Seeing how humans can get out of the hole, grow, and find different meanings that transform their lives even after such a terrible trauma was very powerful.

After the workshop, I gathered my courage and went to speak with Dr. Tedeschi. This may sound like not a big deal for many of you. But I want to highlight the context here. Let's set the stage: we were in Ankara, Türkiye, thousands of miles from the USA. The professor who coined the term post-traumatic growth was standing right in front of a psychology undergrad who was trying to speak English when her native language was Turkish.

Okay, now, just for fun, let's visualize the steps that I took to that stage in the conference hall very slowly, with strong, dramatic music—and me hesitating, maybe even changing my mind for a second, but saying, "Oh, what the hell," and approached him. I just realized that I could have been a writer for telenovelas in another life or maybe in this one, too. Hi Netflix, I'm open to proposals!

An excited squeak escaped my mouth as I cleared my throat to tell him how impressed I was with his research. He looked at me and smiled, humbly thanking me for listening. I told him about my undergraduate thesis[3] (trying to sound all smart :)) and how I would like to continue my graduate studies. He was happy to give me suggestions on what to read and handed me his card so I could reach out to him if I ever ended up across the pond. Four years later, I was in the USA, starting graduate school, and of course, I reached out.

The first time he emailed me back, he said he remembered me (I was thrilled to hear this!). I told him I was in grad school, researching the intersection of positive psychology and family therapy for my master's thesis. I was interested in examining learned optimism as a resiliency-building skill (FYI, we will explore this topic in detail shortly). I also wrote to him that I was often sharing the post-traumatic growth concept with my clients, which has been so helpful and motivating for their healing journey.

And here we are, over twenty years later. People often wonder about how I do what I do as a psychotherapist. They often ask me how I listen to people's problems all day long for so many years. They rarely consider the magic in these conversations where I first see an opening of a new bud of transformation, slowly developing and finally blossoming.

Even after terrible events, witnessing the pain with my clients, standing alongside them, and believing they will continue healing and expanding is so meaningful for me. Observing the post-traumatic growth in my clients is actually how I charge my battery and is part of my chapter five.

CHAPTER 5

---◆◆◆---

Tell Me About Your Childhood!

Not long after my career as a psychotherapist began, I started observing a significant pattern in my clients. The way they connected to the world, the challenges they brought into the therapy room, the tears they shed, the loneliness they felt, the anger they had a hard time managing, and the sadness they couldn't make sense of all had a common thread: their upbringing.

My clients often shared about this unexplainable void that stemmed from their childhood and spilled into adulthood. They have tried many ways to fill this hole but have failed. They kept falling back into it and struggled to get out. They often felt overwhelmed and frustrated. Unfortunately, in the different continents I have lived on, I did not meet many people who could not relate to these experiences at some level.

Meanwhile, I also realized that the stories I was hearing from my clients in the USA were similar to the mother, father, sibling, mother-in-law, boss, and partner struggles I was used to listening to back in Türkiye. Of course, how they dealt with the challenges was tied to different identities and had cultural nuances. Still, overall, I was blown away by how we all want the same things in life: to be seen, heard, loved, understood, and cherished. My heart cracked open.

In these sessions, I observed that how we relate to the world has so much to do with how our caregivers relate to us in childhood. Therefore, even if we think our youth is fine, looking at some of the subtle patterns in our mental software might benefit us if we want to upgrade this inevitable programming. Once familiar with these patterns, we can choose new ways and develop new neural pathways to live a more authentic and vibrant life.

What is Our Programming?

How our caregivers speak to us during our developmental years directly influences our inner voice, which eventually may become our outer voice. Research has shown us that until around age seven, our childhood brainwaves are similar to those we see in an adult's hypnotic state called theta brainwaves[1]. Therefore, in these early years of our development, our brains are like sponges that constantly record the messages from our families, community, and society.

This hypnotic programming directly relates to where we are born and who we most interact with. Our programming becomes our destiny until we process our early experiences, especially the emotionally challenging ones. The good news is that we can always download new information to expand our consciousness and experience the world differently than in the past.

The commonalities in the stories I have had the honor to listen to from my clients brought me back to the research of Dr. John Bowlby and Dr. Mary Ainsworth on attachment theory[2]. This approach conceptualizes these intricate patterns and focuses on attachment security in our external relationships, such as with caregivers or romantic partners.

Throughout the book, I use the terms caregiver and attachment figures interchangeably, and I must also underline that these terms don't necessarily mean only biological parents. Attachment figures can be anyone and everyone who takes care of a child in the early developmental years as guardians or other parental figures.

As we grow into childhood, adolescence, and adulthood, we are deeply influenced by many people who come in and out of our lives, such as friends, teachers, coaches, therapists, mentors, and romantic partners.

It is also important to note the unavoidable effects of the contextual components of our lives, such as race, gender identity, ethnicity, culture, socioeconomic status, sexual orientation, religion, age, mental and physical ability, and many other factors. These variables tremendously impact our experiences and shape who we are, ultimately influencing the journey back to ourselves.

The Attachment Theory Research

Attachment research identifies our caregiver's emotional availability and responsiveness to our needs as substantial contributors to our well-being[3]. While these early bonds can be modified later by peers and other adults in our circle, they stay relatively stable unless there are significant interventions, such as attending psychotherapy, doing other deep inner work, or experiencing life-changing events.

Dear one, why don't we look at pivotal research studies regarding attachment theory to provide more scientific context to our journey

(#nerdalert)? After this chronological timeline of the original attachment theory, we will explore my new conceptualization of the Anxious and Avoidant Parts in detail. So, buckle up your seatbelts; here we go.

Let's start from the very beginning: the Big Bang. Okay, okay, maybe not that far back. One of the first empirical studies on attachment research was "The Strange Situation Experiment," conducted by researchers Dr. Ainsworth and her colleagues during the 1970s[4]. The researchers were interested in observing infants' reactions to their caregivers when a stranger entered the room, and they examined their attachment security. The mother then left the infant in the room alone with the stranger but returned shortly after. These researchers measured the differences in behaviors exhibited when the infants were separated from their caregivers to see if they could find a pattern.

"So, did they find a pattern?" you now might be asking enthusiastically (thanks so much for being so invested). Yes! The researchers concluded that three main attachment styles emerged from their data: **Secure, Avoidant, and Anxious Attachment Styles**, creating the typology model[4].

During this three-minute experiment, **Secure** infants were distressed when their mother left the room but could calm down and continue their play when the mother returned. The **Avoidant** infants were not affected when their mother left the room, and they didn't show distress to the stranger, nor did they give much of a response when the mother reentered the room.

The **Anxious** infants were highly distressed when their mothers left, and they didn't want anything to do with the stranger and showed a more fearful response. Once their mother returned, they had difficulty calming down and could not return to play mode.

Later, another style, the **Disorganized** Attachment Style, was added to the mix[5]. Infants in this particular style had a complicated and unpredictable relationship with their caregivers and didn't show a consistent pattern in their reactions. They sometimes wanted closeness and sometimes rejected it altogether.

Now, let's play some of the infant-caregiver reactions in slow motion. If the relationship between the infant and the caregiver is secure, that means there is safety and trust, right? When left by the caregiver, this infant might cry but has a higher distress tolerance due to the previous secure interactions of feeling safe and protected. There is general trust in the availability of the caregiver. Upon the caregiver's return, the infant reaches for connection and requests the caregiver's soothing.

If the caregiver responds sensitively and attentively, the trust is reinforced, and the infant calms down. The secure relationship makes exploring the world possible, and the interactions feel calm and, at times, fun. They can now see what toys are out there, which friends they can play with, and how to discover the environment and the people around them. They may look back and see if the caregiver is there and know they can return to find what they need. It's a beautiful caregiver-child connection.

You might be wondering how these childhood attachment patterns have anything to do with us now as adults. What are your thoughts on how those interactions between the attachment figure and the infant may translate to how we interact as adults in romantic relationships? Do you think these patterns would follow us into adulthood?

Subsequent research by Drs. Hazan and Shaver, in the 1980s, explored these exact questions[6]. And guess what the answer was? (Drum roll, please.) Yes, similar attachment behaviors were found in adults in their studies. (Yay! You were right!) In other words, the relationship quality with our attachment figures significantly influences our adult attachment types. And just for fun, please re-read the paragraph of the slow-motion *Secure* movie above, but this time, insert two adults in a romantic relationship and see how that sounds.

Since there is always more research to do, and there are many people in academia (#nerdpower) curious about these questions (yay! I'm not alone!), another way of measuring adult attachment styles was created by Drs. Bartholomew and Horowitz in the early 1990s. These researchers focused on the anxiety and avoidance dimensions that formed the four attachment styles: **Secure, Preoccupied, Dismissing, and Fearful**[7].

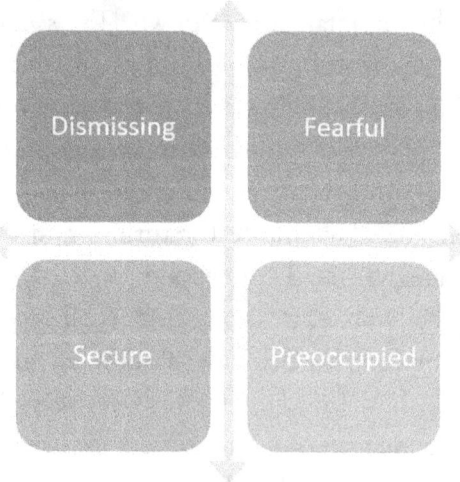

In this two-dimensional model, results indicated that individuals who received lower scores on both anxiety and avoidance dimensions were considered to have a ***Secure Attachment Style***. Individuals who are in this category tend to think that the world is a safe and dependable place. They exhibit trust in both others and themselves, demonstrating responsiveness, sensitivity, and attentiveness to those around them.

Individuals who scored higher on anxiety and lower on avoidance dimensions had a *Preoccupied Attachment Style*. They were found to have a negative view of themselves and feel unworthy or unlovable. They have difficulty trusting that others will be there for them, affecting their relationships and making them afraid of abandonment. They strive for intimacy but have difficulty regulating their emotions when they perceive rejection, which also gets in the way of forming intimacy.

Individuals scoring higher in the avoidance dimension and lower in the anxiety dimension exhibit a *Dismissing Attachment Style*. They often maintain a distance from others due to discomfort with intimacy. Whether through direct avoidance or sending mixed messages, they create distance between themselves and others, making them emotionally unavailable to their partners. They have a hard time identifying and expressing their feelings and needs.

Finally, individuals revealing both high avoidance and high anxiety, characterized by a *Fearful Attachment Style*, harbor a fear of rejection while simultaneously feeling dependent on others. They often struggle with trusting others, leading to considerable distress in their relationships. Just like pressing both the brakes and the gas in a car simultaneously, these individuals desire closeness even as they fear intimacy.

Moving Towards a Spectrum Thinking

While exploring differences in attachment styles can be helpful, life's complexity extends beyond categorizing eight billion people into four boxes (styles). Since each of the anxiety and avoidance dimensions has different shades, I don't think it is productive to pigeonhole ourselves into one box (style) and feel stuck there. How can we foster diversity and inclusion?

In my clinical practice, I've shifted towards viewing attachment security as a spectrum, revealing itself across diverse variations. We all exhibit characteristics from both dimensions, reflecting varying degrees of our Anxious and Avoidant Parts. This perspective shift can aid in understanding the intricacies of our psyches and embracing our unique position on the attachment security continuum, considering the endless combinations possible. This accepting and compassionate approach allows us to perceive each individual as a precious being awaiting discovery. As Rumi wisely advises, all is well and welcome in this approach.

In addition to the psychological excavation of our past, we also need to consider our neurobiology's role in early childhood interactions with our attachment figures further to conceptualize the formation of our Anxious and Avoidant Parts. The nervous system co-regulation (or lack thereof) between the caregiver and the child is crucial in developing attachment security.

I have heard many stories in my practice confirming similar cycles when my clients share their early attachment injuries with their caregivers. The visual below shows how I conceptualize the process of our survival skills formation that manifests as our Anxious and Avoidant Parts. Of course, we have to remember that this is not a linear process. Life is more complicated than that, and we can observe many combinations. Still, I'm hoping this can give us a starting point to pay more attention to the subtle interactions that can impact us in the long term.

Overwhelming
Life Event

Parts Are
Formed

Not Good
Enough
Nervous
System Co-
regulation
from
Caregivers

Child Can't
Self-
Regulate

Continued
Nervous
System
Dysregulation
in the Child

Child Does
Not Feel Seen,
Heard and
Understood

Acting Out &
Acting In

Responces

Adults Continue
to Utilize
Unskilful
Strategies

Resulting in
Disconnection

The lack of attunement and soothing in these early relationships, most probably due to the nervous system dysregulation of the adult, does not allow the child's nervous system to experience co-regulation so they can learn how to self-regulate. Multiple incidents of these attachment injuries, meaning the interactions where the caregiver could not connect and soothe the child efficiently, eventually create the survival parts.

In other words, the creation of Anxiety and Avoidance Parts enables the child to survive in a challenging environment where adults struggle to manage their own nervous systems and provide adequate support to their children. We will discuss these two parts in-depth in the upcoming chapters.

As children, we are vulnerable and cannot fight back or run away, so we must adapt. This is how we survive difficult experiences. Therefore, it makes sense why we may feel anxious when facing uncertainty, inconsistency, or insecurity and have difficulty calming ourselves down. It is also very understandable why we may avoid feeling our feelings and getting intimate with ourselves if we have experienced neglect, abandonment, and unavailability.

To fit in and cope with this pain, our Anxious and Avoidant Parts often take the driver's seat and utilize internalization and externalization strategies as we try to adapt to the environment. Through internalization (acting in), we turn the pain of being in these environments into inside and often experience depression, anxiety, isolation, self-shame, addiction, and self-harm. With externalization (acting out), we might see the unprocessed emotions as anger outbursts, lack of impulse control, lying, bullying, manipulation, gaslighting, and fighting.

These coping mechanisms might have helped us when we didn't have the knowledge and space to heal, so there is no judgment here, dear one. When we think of these parts' strategies as life jackets that have helped us to survive, we can show ourselves the compassion that we need to begin the process of healing and making different choices.

Let's extend the grace we deserve to ourselves for doing the best we can under our circumstances. With the new information we are gathering, we can shift these dysfunctional patterns and become the cycle breakers in our families and societies.

CHAPTER 6

———— ❧ ————

Unveiling the Denial

Troy, which is close to my home city in Türkiye, is an archeological site that showcases the ruins of a city that has been occupied for 5000 years, including the Trojan War. I remember strolling through the gravel paths and touching the walls built and destroyed by nine different civilizations over the years, each one leaving a layer on top of the other.

Just like the city of Troy, we can also rebuild ourselves time and time again, even after significant traumas. However, we must also learn from our past to ensure that the next layer is created more thoughtfully than the one before it.

History usually repeats itself when it is not reconciled. That's why most psychotherapists ask their clients, "Tell me about your childhood." By excavating our ruins, we can make sense of our past, integrate new perspectives, continue to heal, and construct a new future.

Unfortunately, if the dysfunction is all we know, we might think what we went through wasn't that bad. This attitude feeds denial and doesn't allow proper healing on a personal and societal level. Time is not always enough to heal all wounds.

It is understandable to struggle with traveling back to our childhood and reopening old wounds. This chapter will examine some of the challenging aspects of childhood. To best prepare you for this next step, I want to inform you that we may uncover some heavy emotions.

If you currently do not have the bandwidth to learn about trauma research and reflect on your childhood challenges, you can skip the rest of this chapter for now and return when you're ready and want to learn more. Ultimately, you are the expert on yourself, and I trust you will make the best decision for yourself.

Various factors contribute to our struggles during childhood and adulthood. Even the smallest misattunements in the relationship between a caregiver and a child can cause the Anxious and Avoidant Parts of ourselves to develop and expand. Some common examples of factors that affect attachment security in early childhood include caregivers who are constantly in conflict, use substances, have difficulty regulating their own emotions, have experienced a significant loss, are too busy with life's challenges, are not present, do not know how to validate and reflect their child's emotions, distant or are overly rigid or critical due to perfectionism.

Though the list can go on, please remember that no caregiver is perfect (they also probably had imperfect caregivers, so this is intergenerational). Our caregivers did the best they could, but their best might not have been enough for us. Here, our goal is to look at these interactions from a more objective point of view so we can heal and not repeat the same patterns to ourselves or others.

These types of attachment injuries can make a child feel unheard, unseen, neglected, and abandoned. If caregivers fail to meet their attachment needs consistently, the trust between the child and caregiver gets broken. This can lead to a lack of safety and have long-term impacts in adulthood, especially if the caregivers are often unavailable or unresponsive.

The ACE Study

To explore the scientific evidence of how our childhood experiences affect our adult lives, we will refer to the Adverse Childhood Experiences (ACE) study. I discussed this study with my graduate students while teaching the CDFS 641 Trauma and Recovery in Family Therapy class at Purdue University Northwest.

As an exercise, I asked my students to take the ACE Questionnaire, which can be found online, and answer ten questions with either a "yes" or "no" response. By taking this questionnaire, individuals can calculate their ACE score. Would you mind answering this free questionnaire yourself before we proceed any further?

Even if you scored low on ACE, please stay with me if you are uncertain whether you should continue reading. The remaining section of this chapter is still relevant to you because even a few difficult experiences during childhood or any other challenging interactions not covered in these ten questions can contribute to developing the Anxious and Avoidant Parts. Let's now dive into this groundbreaking study and gain a clear understanding of what these outcomes represent.

Between 1995 and 1997, the Centers for Disease Control and Prevention (CDC) and Kaiser Permanente collected data for the ACE Study from over 17,000 people[1]. This study aimed to investigate how childhood abuse, neglect, and other household dysfunctions affected health and well-being outcomes later in life. Patients who received regular physical exams answered ten questions about the first eighteen years of their lives. The original sample consisted mainly of white individuals (75%) with at least an undergraduate college degree, good health insurance, and jobs.

The prevalence of the ten categories that they gathered from the data[1]:

(1) emotional abuse at 11%,
(2) physical abuse at 28%,
(3) sexual abuse at 21%,
(4) mother treated violently at 13%,
(5) substance abuse in the household at 27%,
(6) mental illness in the home at 19%,
(7) parental separation or divorce at 23%,
(8) an incarcerated household member at 5%,
(9) emotional neglect at 15%, and
(10) physical neglect at 10%.

Notice what's happening in you as you see how widespread these instances are. Can you see that these adverse experiences might not be as rare as we think? My heart skipped a beat when I first learned about these numbers.

To recap: nearly 30% of this sample was physically abused as children, almost 30% lived with someone with a substance abuse problem in the household, and an astonishing number of one in five was sexually abused before the age of 18. When we look at the big picture, results indicated that 64% of the sample had at least one

ACE score. The statistics become even more distressing when I read that 1 in 11 of us has a 6+ ACE score. Wow!

The original ACE study has been replicated many times since then. One of the largest of these studies was conducted between 2011 and 2020. Researchers collected data from 264,882 individuals from 50 states, representing a more diverse sample[2]. The findings once again highlighted the high prevalence of childhood adversity:

- 34% of participants experiencing emotional abuse,
- 23% of participants experiencing physical abuse,
- 27% of participants experiencing household substance abuse,
- 64% reporting at least one ACE, and
- 17% reporting four or more ACEs.

Now, let's take some deep breaths, shall we? As a society, we are often in denial about the frequency of these unhealthy patterns. Family is labeled as a sacred word, regardless of the dysfunctionality. This unquestioning family loyalty is one of the main reasons why the cycle of dysfunctionality repeats from generation to generation.

We tend to deny or minimize such issues and then sweep them under the rug, believing that time will heal all wounds. This denial only leads to storing all these experiences in our minds and bodies until they become too much to handle. Books like *The Body Keeps the Score* by Dr. Bessel van der Kolk[3] and *The Body Remembers* by Babette Rothschild[4] offer fantastic insights into the mental, emotional, and physical effects of these experiences for those who want to delve deeper.

I vividly remember the first time I showed my graduate students the graphs about the relationship between ACE scores and different health problems and risk behaviors in adulthood. I will never forget their shocked reactions when they saw the increasing percentages of these problems with the corresponding ACE scores one chart after another.

Over 40 outcomes all showed the exact correlation, and every time, the higher the ACE score, the worse the outcome. These results proved that higher ACE scores correlated with a higher prevalence of smoking, COPD (chronic obstructive pulmonary disease), obesity, teen sexual behaviors, teen pregnancy, STDs, attempted suicide, lifetime history of depression, as well as a higher risk of being a victim of domestic violence, perpetrating domestic violence, being sexually assaulted as an adult, HIV/AIDS, alcoholism, dependency on prescription drugs like antidepressants, anti-anxiety meds, anti-psychotics, and work-related problems[1].

Dr. Felitti's article titled "The Relation Between Adverse Childhood Experiences and Adult Health: Turning Gold into Lead" discusses the long-lasting impact of ACE scores[5]. According to these findings:

- A male child with a **six** ACE score is **4,600%** more likely to use injection drugs later in life than a male child with no ACE score.
- An individual with **four or more** ACE scores is **460%** more likely to experience depression and has a **1220%** increase in suicide attempts compared to someone with no ACE score.

Additional findings have supported the notion that early adverse childhood experiences have significant negative effects. The results indicate that:

- Those with an ACE score of **four or more** are **400%** more likely to develop alcoholism[6],
- There is a significant increase in smoking as the ACEs increase[7] and
- An increase of **62%** in the number of non-medical use of prescription drugs for each ACE score[8].

I want to share one final result with you involving life expectancy, so take a deep breath. Now, imagine one of your classmates from high school. Let's say she/he/they do not have any ACE scores, which statistically makes their expected death around 79. In contrast, your other classmate who scores a six or more on the ACE questionnaire is statistically likely to die around 60. The adverse childhood experiences steal nearly 20 years of one's life[9]. Just like that. How is your heart right now? Mine is very tight, and there's a lump in my throat.

Reading these results from the ACE study made me sad and heartbroken for myself, my family, my friends, and my community. The reality is that the majority of us have some ACEs. My mind then immediately went to calculating the millions of people struggling with these challenges, not just in our neighborhood, state, or country but all around the world as well.

Now, we can see the profound impact of childhood trauma on our development into adulthood. Every one of these scores is an attachment injury. Unfortunately, when the attachment security in the house where we are supposed to be cared for and protected is ruptured, our attachment to ourselves and the world is also ruptured.

When our early attachment security is compromised, it extends beyond the home, affecting our connection with ourselves and the broader world. Growing up in an unsafe environment may lead us to generalize and perceive the world as a whole as unsafe. We might live a fear-based life that feels like a familiar home. Further, we might encounter unsafe people who will make us feel that familiar dysfunction later in life. This is why creating safety and security within ourselves can help us make different choices instead of our trauma responses and lead to a different future aligned with our values.

It's Not Only ACEs

Let's not forget that many other difficult life experiences leave a mark on our psyche, such as a worldwide pandemic, social justice issues, community violence, terrorism, natural disasters, accidents, bullying, school violence, losses, intimate partner violence, and war. In addition to our lived experiences, epigenetics research provides evidence of intergenerational transmission of trauma[10]. Being human means being exposed to suffering; no one is immune to this reality.

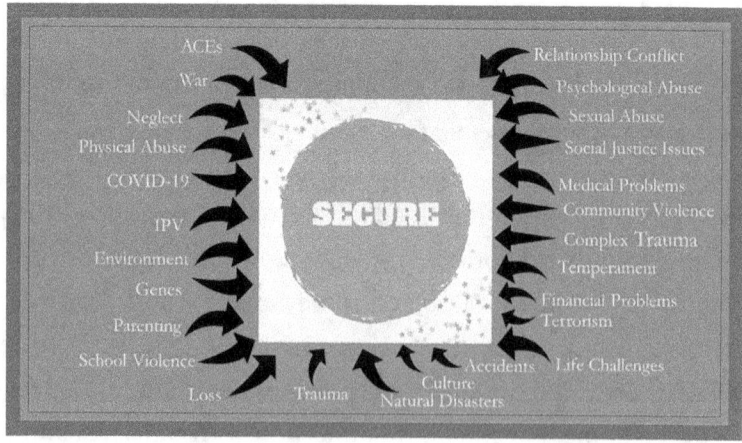

Yes, we might not be able to go back in time and erase our traumatic experiences, but we can look at how we adapted to be able to survive. We can notice that these adaptations are the Anxious and Avoidant Parts that were formed to cope with the world.

With this knowledge and awareness, we can transform the unhelpful adaptations into a newly constructed future. I'm not saying it is easy, but staying stuck in pain isn't easy either. This is where we begin, and we will do this together.

While reading more about the Anxious and Avoidant Parts in the following two chapters, I encourage you to notice how you relate to yourself when each part is activated and gets in the driver's seat of your life. Gently listen to how each part presents itself in your inner world, what it is telling you, how it is trying to help you, and what it is trying to achieve. These unique parts hold messages waiting for us to hear and understand. The key to our healing is to appreciate and honor these messages constructively. What was unsaid needs to be heard.

CHAPTER 7

Meeting our Anxious Part

Now that we have explored the causes and conditions that lead to the formation of Anxious and Avoidant Parts, how about we get to know them better so we can welcome, befriend, and heal them with our *Secure Self*?

Great, let's start by exploring how much space our Anxious Part occupies in our psyche by taking the questionnaire below. Of course, this is not a constant and can change with intentional effort. Let's look at how our inner forecast is right now with (1) representing 'strongly disagree' and (5) representing 'strongly agree'.

In the next section, we will learn different *Inner Security* tools to regulate our emotions more effectively when these parts take over. For now, we are focusing on getting to know these parts better without judgment and extending compassion.

	(1)	(2)	(3)	(4)	(5)
(1) I have a hard time trusting the intelligence within myself.	○	○	○	○	○
(2) I don't like sitting with my thoughts, feelings, and body sensations.	○	○	○	○	○
(3) I'm not good enough.	○	○	○	○	○
(4) I have a hard time accepting myself as I am.	○	○	○	○	○
(5) It is hard for me to motivate myself.	○	○	○	○	○
(6) I am not worthy of love and support.	○	○	○	○	○
(7) I don't like trying new things.	○	○	○	○	○
(8) I have a hard time calming myself.	○	○	○	○	○
(9) My inner critic quickly takes over.	○	○	○	○	○
(10) I often judge my feelings.	○	○	○	○	○
(11) I keep myself busy all the time.	○	○	○	○	○

	(1)	(2)	(3)	(4)	(5)
(12) I struggle with change.	○	○	○	○	○
(13) I have a hard time seeing the broader perspective.	○	○	○	○	○
(14) I am not compassionate with myself.	○	○	○	○	○
(15) I have a hard time being in the present.	○	○	○	○	○
(16) I don't listen to my intuition.	○	○	○	○	○
(17) I have a hard time recognizing my strengths.	○	○	○	○	○
(18) I don't like to be just by myself.	○	○	○	○	○
(19) I have a hard time getting my needs met.	○	○	○	○	○
(20) I don't have many inner resources.	○	○	○	○	○
(21) I am anxious.	○	○	○	○	○

Let's check in for a minute here. What did you notice about how much the Anxious Part takes charge of your life? Please take a deep breath and trust that this part has more of an intention to protect you, not to harm you. Together, we will find more effective ways to honor that intention. But first, why not explore how the Anxious Part presents itself with the help of my client's story?

As soon as we started our session, Sonia looked at me, shaking her head, and said, "I'm so pissed off at myself!" She took a sip from her water bottle. There were no lemons in it this time as she regularly had, meaning she was in her "rabbit hole," which was how she referred to her dark place.

"I'm tired," she said. "I'm tired of trying. I'm tired of trying to eat healthy, exercise, meditate, keep my stress level down, and continue with my life. I'm tired of it all. The future is so uncertain. I'm not sure if my husband can keep the business running after all this or if we can even make the mortgage. I didn't imagine all this happening before we moved to this new house. I'm also worried about our parents' health back home. Everything is very overwhelming. I couldn't handle it yesterday, so I lay in bed while my husband took the kids for a walk. It was just like the old days when I was so anxious," she looked down.

"Whatever I tried to do, it was this feeling, this voice telling me that I was not doing the right thing, not being the best mom, wife, daughter, teacher, and all the other roles I have. I'm not enough. I could feel all this in my chest. I couldn't breathe and felt caged. I didn't want to think or try anymore. The worry was overwhelming, and, of course, the intense anxiety arrived. I felt like I was having a heart attack and was scared. I know I shouldn't feel this way. I have a lot to be grateful for, so there's definitely something wrong with me.

I just can't handle the pressures of life anymore." Sonia's Anxious Part was in full force.

She took another sip from her water bottle and looked at me, waiting for me to say something. I assume she was waiting for me to disapprove of her choices or tell her that she should have encouraged herself to go for a walk or to call a supportive friend.

Instead, I looked at her and said, "You're so brave, and I'm proud of you." Tears immediately began streaming down from her eyes, her big, brown, beautiful eyes. She couldn't say anything back. She was filled with surprise as if she was waiting to be criticized. But all she wanted was to be seen. And I saw her. I saw how hard she was trying.

I had been meeting with Sonia for the last several months, starting to untangle the challenges from her past. Sonia, an elementary school teacher, came to see me, hoping to calm her anxiety. She had multiple miscarriages and was having difficulty being present with her two kids. The losses she experienced, unfortunately, were not previously adequately addressed. (Special thanks to our cultures that don't know how to cope with grief!) She still was carrying the heavy burden. She was in much pain, and on top of all that, like millions of other people, she was affected by the pandemic, its residual effects, and the wars that touched her personally.

We watched two different movies during her sessions. The one she watched was a black-and-white film filled with trauma, and the one I watched was a documentary about an incredibly resilient woman learning how to relate to herself more compassionately.

"Why did you just say that?" she finally asked.

"Because, Sonia, you're doing everything you can. I'm so impressed by your willingness to heal and expand your heart. You are trying to understand the patterns that don't serve you well anymore and respond in healthier ways. And we've been working on the pressure of perfectionism in which you were raised. I can hear that you sometimes speak to yourself from that perspective."

She was listening and starting to breathe. "The good news is that you don't need to be perfect anymore," I continued. "It is okay not to be okay, and maybe we can work on how to respond to yourself compassionately when you have bad days like this. How does that sound?" She nodded her head. Her tears were taking a break. The younger part within her, often called the Inner Child in Transactional Analysis, began to find a sense of calm. This was something new for her.

Sonia did not grow up in an abusive home; however, the perfectionist expectations imposed significant pressure on her during her formative years. Due to her caregivers' lack of consistent co-regulation in her childhood, she struggled with regulating her nervous system. Unfortunately, this resulted in her difficulty providing co-regulation to her children's nervous systems. If she didn't learn to break the cycle of intergenerational transmission of anxiety, her children might also suffer. I often told her that healing our Inner Child helps heal our children. Reparenting our Inner Child is the best gift we can give our loved ones.

When the Anxious Part struggles with heightened emotions, it needs to be soothed with attuned compassion. We can think about this part as a manifestation of the older experiences of anxiety but arising in the current time. Older childhood wounds may have been touched if our reactions to the recent event exceed our typical responses.

The folder in our mind's desktop then opens up, and we might be responding to the combination of older and current injuries. Let's say on a scale of 0-10, our reaction is a seven. This may mean that our previous baggage might cause four out of the seven, while the current situation only deserves a three response. Therefore, when activated this much, we need to regulate our nervous system before responding.

When the Anxious Part takes over due to the present injuries, our bodies unconsciously re-live the past experiences that remind us of the current situation, especially from our younger years. This is how our past becomes present. In these moments, we can learn to provide good enough reparenting to our Inner Child so they have a different life experience now and can heal. (If you are wondering how we do this reparenting, stay tuned. In the next section, we will practice specific skills for the compassionate reparenting process together as a critical *Inner Security* tool.)

What's Happening in Our Brain?

When her Anxious Part took over, Sonia often talked to herself from a fear-based mindset. In these moments, our limbic system, the emotion center of our brain, is activated, and we see the world as a place of unsafety. When fear is in full force, we might catastrophize and believe the worst-case scenario. In these moments, Sonia often focused on what was lacking instead of focusing on her needs, and she tried to fix things or people outside her control, which often resulted in disappointment and heartache.

Neurobiologically, our amygdala (remember the smoke detector?) begins to hijack the pre-frontal cortex, the most developed part of our brain capable of perceiving the big picture and employing coping skills[1]. The prefrontal cortex oversees our executive functions and language skills. However, accessing this part becomes challenging when our sympathetic system (fight/flight/freeze/fawn) is activated. We face difficulties considering different options and can't think clearly (insert the destructive reactions we all struggle with).

Learning to befriend our nervous system will be crucial in our healing journey. I often use a world-renowned psychiatrist, Dr. Daniel Siegel's hand metaphor[2], to bring some neuroscience to our sessions (#nerdalert). Sonia appreciated these scientific explanations and said they helped her normalize the process and avoid shame.

Dr. Siegel, in his hand model, describes our arm as representing the brain stem (reptilian part), the palm and thumb as the limbic system (mammalian part), and the top of knuckles as representing the prefrontal lobe (human part). When we are grounded and calm, all three parts of our brain are connected and integrated, and our lid is down (knuckles clenched).

When our emotions are activated by being anxious, threatened, or overwhelmed, the limbic system takes charge, and the connection to the prefrontal lobe is cut off; in other words, our lid is off (now the fist is open and disconnected from the thumb and the palm). In this place, we primarily function from only the mammalian and reptilian parts of our brain and do not have access to the more developed region[1]. This explains why we say or do stupid things when all worked up. (Been there, done that!)

Before making sound decisions, we need to learn to reconnect the prefrontal part of our brain with the other regions (visualize the fingers forming back into a fist). Does that make sense to you? Oh, no, now I imagine a bunch of people reading this book making weird hand gestures. Maybe it may be helpful to search for "Dan Siegel hand model" on YouTube and listen to it directly from him[2] :)

Sonia and I discussed ways to get her lid down and secure. Once she understood the underlying mechanisms in her reactions, she was more open to investigating some useful regulation tools.

Calming our nervous system can be accomplished by vagus nerve stimulation techniques. By stimulating the vagus nerve, we activate our parasympathetic nervous system, which is responsible for rest and digestion, ultimately creating a calmer mind.

The vagus nerve is the longest cranial nerve in our nervous system[3]. It carries information to and from our body and the brain. It can be stimulated to reduce anxiety in many ways, such as deep breathing[4], cold exposure (drinking cold water, cold shower, or splashing cold water on the face)[5], humming[6], singing[6], chanting[6], yoga[7], t'ai chi[8] massage[9], meditation[10], exercise[11] laughing[12], and acupuncture[13]. Increased vagal tone is associated with positive emotions and better physical health[14].

I often work with my clients to build tools for their nervous system needs so that they can move from red to yellow to green zone, just like the traffic light. For example, when Sonia felt herself slipping into the yellow zone, she chose a *Yoga with Adriene*[15] video on YouTube (I absolutely adore her work). She practiced some yoga and meditation to return to the present moment.

The next time Sonia felt that she was going to have an anxiety attack (red), she held ice cubes in her hands and was able to calm her nervous system down (slowly to yellow and then green). Cold exposure directly activates the parasympathetic nervous system, slowing our heart and breathing rate[5]. Several of my clients used this trick even when doing job interviews in Zoom while holding ice cubes and regulating their lids. In case you are wondering, yes, they got the jobs :).

Sonia also loved technology, so I informed her about HeartMath Institute[16] and their work on heart rate variability to calm the nervous system. Heart rate variability and vagal tone are found to be positively correlated[17.] The EmWave device I got about ten years ago measured the pulse through the fingertip to give feedback about your heart rhythm so that you can use the data to balance your physiological state with steady breathing. Backed by thirty years of research, they now have more updated versions that I recommend you check out[18].

I also told Sonia about the Muse headbands[19], which uses electroencephalogram (EEG) technology to measure the electrical activity in our brains. These headbands are worn while meditating, and you can see and hear immediate feedback about what is happening in your brain. When your mind is calm, you are rewarded by hearing the birds chirping. You can collect more bird points by slowing your breath and heart rate, so it's fun, too. With this tool, you train your brain with biofeedback and practice getting your lid down.

On the journey of cultivating *Inner Security*, we need as much support as possible. In addition to our therapeutic work, I encouraged Sonia to explore the twelve-step program called ACA (Adult Children of Alcoholics and Dysfunctional Families) to heal in a community. This is an organization that started for only adult members of families with alcoholism but then expanded to help those from any dysfunctional family system. Many of us come from some shade of dysfunction in our family of origin and can benefit from finding additional support from ACA (https://adultchildren. org/)[20]. You can begin by reading their laundry list to see if you find anything that you can relate to: https://adultchildren.org/literature/laundry-list/[21].

Sonia slowly learned how to reparent her Inner Child and started having a more compassionate relationship with herself. She practiced regulating her unpleasant emotions triggered by the Anxious Part by welcoming them so she could hear their messages. Remember Rumi's words? She used them as her lighthouse.

Sonia also realized that the remedy for calming down the Anxious Part is to provide herself with the opposite of the inconsistency, unavailability, and gaslighting she received in her childhood. She got so much better at stimulating her vagus nerve and having her lid down more frequently. She began letting her *Secure Self* provide the consistency, availability, compassion, validation, encouragement, understanding, and predictability she needed, which you will be practicing soon.

When Sonia made peace with her Anxious Part and let her *Secure Self* guide her, she also started trusting the intelligence within herself. She could be able to sit with her thoughts, feelings, and body sensations and calm her nervous system down. She realized she was good enough and worthy of love and support. First, she started accepting herself as she was, and then she could be able to motivate herself to expand.

Sonia started trying new things, welcomed change, and noticed the broader perspective of life. She gave herself breaks just to be, got rest, was more present with herself, and spent time alone. She became more compassionate with herself and focused on her needs. As a result, she was calmer and more present with her loved ones, too.

She began recognizing her strengths, listening to her intuition, building other inner resources, and feeling *Inner Security*. It has been my pleasure to witness her transformation, and when you are done reading this book, you will also have a blueprint of how to do this, just like Sonia.

Let's end this chapter with a practice that will allow you to get closer to your Anxious Part. This will take some imagination and being able to wear the shoes of the Anxious Part. What would it say to you if you could connect to this part of yourself and give a voice to it?

Connection Practice

Please write a letter from the voice of your Anxious Part to yourself, expressing all the thoughts and feelings it carries. This is a free-flow practice, so there is no right or wrong answer. Get into the mindset of the Anxious Part for a few minutes and give a voice to this part. This part has important things to say to you. How is it wanting you to protect yourself? What does it want you to achieve? What is it afraid of? What are its concerns? What are its intentions?

Start with "Dear _____" (insert your name) and end it with "Love You, The Anxious Part."

CHAPTER 8

Meeting Our
Avoidant Part

Let's spend some time exploring the Avoidant Part of our psyche. Together, we can reflect on how our emotions, thoughts, and behaviors present themselves when this part of us takes over, with (1) representing 'strongly disagree' and (5) representing 'strongly agree'. This self-reflection can help us find ways to improve our ability to connect with ourselves and the world from a more *Secure place*.

	(1)	(2)	(3)	(4)	(5)
(1) I don't feel connected to the higher intelligence within myself.	○	○	○	○	○
(2) I don't like being emotional.	○	○	○	○	○

	(1)	(2)	(3)	(4)	(5)
(3) I don't like conflict.	○	○	○	○	○
(4) I don't need to comfort myself.	○	○	○	○	○
(5) I avoid taking healthy risks.	○	○	○	○	○
(6) I do not need soothing.	○	○	○	○	○
(7) I don't like trying new things.	○	○	○	○	○
(8) I can't trust my emotions.	○	○	○	○	○
(9) I don't need help to achieve my goals.	○	○	○	○	○
(10) I find it challenging to identify my own feelings.	○	○	○	○	○
(11) I keep myself busy instead of dwelling on emotions.	○	○	○	○	○
(12) I don't spend time thinking about setbacks in life.	○	○	○	○	○

	(1)	(2)	(3)	(4)	(5)
(13) I am not interested in other's perspectives.	○	○	○	○	○
(14) I am not compassionate with myself.	○	○	○	○	○
(15) I don't allow my feelings to guide me in life.	○	○	○	○	○
(16) I have a hard time identifying my strengths.	○	○	○	○	○
(17) I don't feel connected to my intuition.	○	○	○	○	○
(18) I only enjoy being on my own.	○	○	○	○	○
(19) I am not sure what my needs are.	○	○	○	○	○
(20) I don't have many internal resources.	○	○	○	○	○
(21) I am avoidant.	○	○	○	○	○

How was that experience for you? While answering the questions above, what feelings, thoughts, and body sensations did you notice arising? Let's approach this part with love and compassion as we explore this further. Please take a deep breath and trust that this part of you has good intentions and the capability to figure out more skillful ways to honor these intentions. The Avoidant Part aims to keep you safe, ensure your survival, and help you succeed. However, its ways of connecting to the world may no longer be useful and need to be replaced with more effective ways.

When our Avoidant Part takes control of our lives, we may have thoughts such as, "Why would I want to feel uncomfortable emotions when I can just avoid them? What's the point anyway? The past is behind me, so there's no need to dwell on it. I should just move on and focus on positive vibes. Life is too short to waste on negative feelings."

Untangling the impact of the Avoidant Part might be tricky. On the outside, it may seem like we are simply trying to avoid conflict and discomfort. We may choose not to express our feelings or assert our needs to avoid upsetting others. This can manifest as people-pleasing behaviors as we want everyone to get along, even at the cost of intimacy and deep connection.

We may also distance ourselves from others, withdrawing or dismissing them entirely, as it can be challenging to trust those around us. However, without trust, we cannot live genuinely or authentically.

On the inside, when the Avoidant Part takes over, we tend to shut ourselves off from experiencing negative emotions. We resist feeling grief, anger, disappointment, frustration, or sadness and prefer to ignore them. But as Buddhists say, "What we resist persists."

This attitude makes it challenging for us to process our emotions around tough life experiences like the pandemic, job loss, relationship problems, breakups, divorce, or losing a loved one. In fact, it may even seem like a waste of time to deal with our feelings in these situations.

As the Avoidant Part takes more charge of our lives, we may find it challenging to acknowledge our emotions and fulfill our needs. This can lead to further discomfort, which we may not even be aware of. As a result, our ability to self-regulate becomes even more challenging, as our nervous systems have already been through enough and cannot handle further dysregulation.

This is where addictions come into play as we look for ways to numb the pain. To avoid this agony, we may turn to food, alcohol, relationships, drugs, sex, video games, pornography, work, social media, tobacco, shopping, or any other means that provide a short-lived, false sense of comfort. It's not easy to be human, that's for sure.

The Avoidant Part is a common topic that surfaces during therapy sessions in my practice. After settling on the brown couch in my office, Miguel sighed heavily and said, "I don't know where to start." He appeared weary.

"I'm sick of not measuring up," he went on. "I feel like I'm doing everything I can but still not making anyone happy. My husband keeps telling me I'm not listening to him, and he feels lonely. My boss says I need to start considering managing the team at the firm, which entails taking on more leadership responsibilities and stress. Additionally, my family needs more support with my mother's illness." He looked down, and it was clear why he was feeling exhausted; he was carrying a lot of weight on his shoulders.

Miguel, a successful investment banker, sought guidance in managing the stress in his life. Our relationship began with the EAP sessions (employee assistance program) he was referred to through his work. Still, he decided to stay in therapy when he realized that not much could be resolved in only six sessions (I mean, I'm good, but not that good!).

There are rarely quick fixes to our deep-rooted challenges. I initially informed him that I had yet to find the magic solution to make everything better immediately despite my meticulous search across several continents. Our relationship was based on honesty, realistic expectations, and, of course, some sarcasm. I knew we would get along well when he told me that his favorite character on *Friends* was Chandler.

"A voice in my head constantly says that I should do better. It just doesn't accept things as they are, and nothing I do is good enough," he added.

I was blown away. Despite only having worked together for a couple of months, I was impressed by his ability to articulate the inner workings of his psyche. "Wow, Miguel," I said. "I'm not sure if this had been something I would have heard from you before. Seeing how you are becoming clearer about what is happening in your mind is amazing. I believe this might help you to decide how you want to move forward." This time, Miguel took the compliment more comfortably; he was starting to trust the therapy process.

During our conversation, we discussed how our Anxious and Avoidant Parts often take control of our lives, especially during stressful times. I often asked him to identify which part he was responding to life from, and he would frequently say that the Avoidant Part was in charge. Through our work, Miguel began to realize how he had learned at a young age about how the world worked and how he had been conditioned to ignore his needs.

If our caregivers do not see, hear, or understand us adequately, we may feel ignored and unloved. Even though we want to be close to them, it can be painful to do so. It can feel like we are touching a hot stove over and over again. If trying to get close means hurting, why would we want to do that? Of course, we will learn to be distant and not get intimate. We will learn to be self-reliant so we don't bother anyone. We will quickly understand that our caregivers' needs surpass everybody else's, conditioning us to suppress our needs.

Many of my clients, including Miguel, have reported that while growing up, they often heard phrases like "I'll give you something to cry about," "Oh, come on, it wasn't that bad," "No need to dwell on it," "Get over it already," "It wasn't that big of a deal anyway," "This stuff happens in all families," "You are too sensitive," or "What's wrong with you? Just move on." These messages eventually create an environment that lacks intimacy and authenticity.

Through these types of interactions in childhood, a child may begin to learn negative beliefs, such as:

- "I am on my own,"
- "I am not lovable,"
- "I am not good enough,"
- "I can't trust my emotions,"
- "People are not there for me,"
- "It's not safe to feel emotions and have needs,"
- "There must be something wrong with me to feel this way,"
- "The world is not a safe place; I always need to protect myself," and
- "My perceptions are not correct, so I should always doubt myself."

These beliefs can prevent the child from learning the importance of interdependent relationships. Even if the damage was not intentional, it may be impactful.

Over time, these learned beliefs and behaviors may make us excessively self-reliant, frequently putting aside our feelings. We stop paying attention to our own needs and start building walls. Gradually, this distancing behavior becomes effortless, leading to a reluctance to form close connections with oneself and others. Eventually, this avoidance becomes our default mode, and we start associating it with a sense of comfort and familiarity.

Sometimes, we may desire this familiarity in our relationships without even realizing it. However, this can often lead us to end up in relationships where we feel invisible, unheard, and unloved. We might wonder how we ended up where we are.

This cycle can become a dark hole we repeatedly fall into. It may be difficult to believe that intimacy can be safe until we have corrective experiences. For instance, therapy, reparenting, or other attuned interactions can help us trust and feel safe in our relationships.

What's Happening in Our Minds?

To facilitate the healing process, I asked, "Would you be willing to try a unique exercise to work with this critical voice, Miguel?" I wanted him to practice a tool from Gestalt therapy to identify and communicate with his Avoidant Part. Miguel smiled and nodded in agreement.

"I want you to talk to your Avoidant Part for a few minutes. Imagine the Avoidant Part is sitting on a chair in front of you. I know it's a bit unconventional to talk to a voice in a chair," I said.

"What am I supposed to say?" he asked.

"It's up to you," I replied.

After a few moments, Miguel looked at the imaginary Avoidant Part and began to speak to the chair. "I don't like you. You make my life miserable. You create this distance within me and with others. You don't allow me to feel my feelings, and you try to suppress them. But the more I slide the shit under the carpet, the more it smells. I don't want you in my life anymore. F*ck off!"

He looked at me like he was waiting for a grade. "How was that?" I asked.

"Felt good. It was freeing to get it out," he answered.

"Ok, now I'd like you to write down what this Avoidant Part tells you when it shows up in your life," I said, handing him a piece of paper. "You can write it in whichever format you'd like. Some prefer writing in paragraphs, and some prefer bullet points or any other way you can think of," I ended. His long list came about very fast since he was familiar with this type of inner talk, which I call "the old radio station."

After Miguel finished his list, I asked him to read it as if he was telling it to his best friend, Ethan. Miguel looked confused. I gave him my "You know my weird ways by now" look with a smile. He knew that "look" well and went along with it. I asked him to imagine Ethan next to him and read the whole list to him. Unfortunately, the list was full of insults, put-downs, disrespectful responses to failures, discouraging comments, and cruel criticisms.

When I asked him how he felt about the exercise, he replied that he would never speak to Ethan like that and that his stomach was upset to see that this was the radio station playing in his mind. I didn't have to say much after that in the session because the best realizations in therapy are when my clients come to conclusions themselves.

In later therapy sessions, we incorporated various *Inner Security* tools to improve the Avoidant Part's ability to connect better with the world. Unfortunately, many of us didn't learn how to express our feelings adequately during childhood, which explains why we struggle with identifying and communicating them as adults.

To help Miguel with this challenge, I suggested using "The Feelings Wheel," a helpful tool developed by Dr. Gloria Willcox that we often use in therapy[1]. This colorful wheel displays a range of common emotions, allowing us to quickly identify the ones we're experiencing.

I further explained to him that labeling our feelings helps calm down our limbic system, as it engages the Broca region in the frontal cortex of our brain[2]. Miguel also appreciated learning about the neuroscience behind our work together.

From the feelings wheel, Miguel identified feeling frustrated and discouraged as his current mood. We talked about when he felt like this and how he tended to shut down and isolate himself from others. It was his way of protecting himself from further pain. Although it may not be the healthiest coping mechanism, it made sense, given the circumstances of his childhood.

Healing requires us to accept and love ourselves, including how we cope with life's pressures. It's okay to feel overwhelmed and have a trauma response. We are all human and cannot control what life throws at us or when we get triggered. However, we can focus on what we can control, such as regulating our nervous system to bring ourselves back to the present moment.

Miguel learned to recognize and accept his feelings without judgment as he began practicing meditation and reflecting on his inner experiences. He started getting closer to himself. With continued practice, he became better at identifying his emotions more effectively, especially when feeling overwhelmed. He realized it was easier to name and express his feelings when his lid was down, so he worked on his nervous system regulation tools. This helped him to build *Inner Security* and created new neural pathways in his brain.

The next step we worked on together was identifying our needs. Our emotions tell us what we need when we listen to them closely. As for many of us, identifying his needs was challenging for Miguel. In one of our sessions, I recommended utilizing the "Feelings and Needs Inventory" from The Center for Nonviolent Communication[3].

I frequently would ask Miguel how he was feeling, which he would choose from the feelings wheel, and then what he needed, which he would identify from the needs inventory. In one of those instances, he said, "I feel depleted and withdrawn. I need joy and closeness."

This provided valuable insight and allowed us to establish concrete steps to help him obtain his needs. As he grew more accustomed to this practice, he started taking a moment throughout the day to ask himself, "What am I feeling right now? What do I need?" This helped him feel more in touch with himself. He even printed out the feelings wheel and the needs inventory and placed them on the fridge as a reminder. I truly appreciated his willingness to improve his self-regulation.

I also encouraged him to join ACA groups to connect with other people going through similar experiences. During this exploration, he realized he could identify what he was currently missing by reflecting on what was missing in his childhood.

Miguel has learned to provide himself with the acceptance, approval, and validation he didn't receive enough of when he was young. He practiced reparenting his Inner Child with unconditional love, compassion, encouragement, and understanding and allowed himself to feel all his feelings (practices on how to do this are coming soon). As a result, he became more emotionally present with himself, his feelings, and his needs, which also helped him connect with his loved ones.

Let's take a moment to reflect on our Avoidant Part before moving on to the next section. This exercise will help us better understand how to work with this part of ourselves and allow our *Secure Self* to heal its wounds.

Connection Practice

Please write a letter from the voice of your Avoidant Part to yourself, expressing all the thoughts and feelings it carries. This is a free-flow practice, so there is no right or wrong answer. Get into the mindset of the Avoidant Part for a few minutes and give a voice to this part. This part has important things to say to you. How is it wanting you to protect yourself? What does it want you to achieve? What is it afraid of? What are its concerns? What are its intentions?

Start with "Dear _____" (insert your name) and end it with "Love You, The Avoidant Part."

Section 2

Inner Security Toolbox

CHAPTER 9

Building Connection to
Our *Secure Self*

During my trip to Costa Rica, I came across a fascinating plant while touring the Sierpe River on a sunny day in the Osa Peninsula. The plant was floating on the river without any visible roots, and it caught my attention. I asked our tour guide, Enoc, about it, and he told me it was a type of water hyacinth. He pulled one out of the water and showed us the inside of the bulb-like stem. To my surprise, it had many air-filled sacs on the inner wall, which kept it afloat. This unique plant had evolved, adapted to the tropical environment, and thrived.

How badass is that? Even if anything happened to some of its air sacs, many more kept it alive and floating on the water. It made me think about how we could learn from it and become more resourceful and adaptive on the inside.

Creating various psychological *Inner Security* tools is like having multiple air sacs that can help us navigate through challenges. When life happens, and some of our air sacs are wounded, we can rely on our other inner resources to continue floating.

Getting to know and spending time with our *Secure Self* is a lifelong exploration. I often tell my clients that this is like learning a new language; it will be uncomfortable and awkward initially, but once you get the hang of it, you will be able to let your *Secure Self* be the guide.

In this journey, you will build *Inner Security* by attending to your needs, wants, and interests and creating a life where you are the best version of yourself. Why not start this journey with a motto I encourage us to use, especially when we feel stuck in life?

If we survived our past, we all have a Secure Self.

Please take a deep breath and let that sink in for a moment. When I perceive I don't have many options or lose connection with the flow of life, I keep repeating myself; "If I survived my past, I have a *Secure Self*. What would my *Secure Self* guide me to do at this moment?"

The reality is if we outlasted our shitty history (of course, the shittiness is a spectrum, and we all have some shit in our past, and only you can decide how shitty it was), we also have a part that kept us going. We have this resiliency that lets us continue our journey in life. We all have a *Secure Self*.

Remember the saying that *it takes a village to raise a child*? Whether we realize it or not, many people and experiences have helped us survive our past. Let's face it; it can be difficult to look at our upbringing objectively and discern, "This worked" and "This didn't work." We might feel like admitting something didn't work is abandoning our caregivers, not being loyal to our lineage, or putting them down when they weren't *that bad*.

I'm sure most of our parents were not *that bad*, and they did their best, but the bottom line is that they probably had some shitty past trauma too. Who can say they've had a perfect upbringing anyway? Either way, there is no blame here. We just need to be honest to heal and look at the pain when we were not adequately seen or heard, which takes much inner courage.

In the first section, we acknowledged the origins of this pain. We highlighted other challenging life experiences outside of our family of origin as contributors to the formation of Anxious and Avoidant Parts.

In this section, we will take responsibility for our present choices. We will figure out what we need to do to break the transmission chain of pain and help the next generations have a less shitty past.

Our focus will be on cultivating optimism and self-compassion and identifying our strengths. We will learn to be our own secure base and safe haven and practice reparenting our Inner Child. Finally, we will practice letting our *Secure Self* guide us and take care of the Anxious and Avoidant Parts, which will result in experiencing *Inner Security*.

On a side note, if you haven't watched it yet, the Netflix series "Another Self" is an excellent example of how trauma is passed down through generations and how people can heal from it[1]. The story takes place on Cunda Island, Türkiye, where my grandparents had their house, and I used to spend every summer. Seeing my childhood home in the show was a real treat, and I hope you'll enjoy it too.

Now, think about the people in your village that supported you. I am specifically asking about the ones who helped and contributed to your *well-being*. Some qualities that create a secure relationship can be described as loving, embracing, engaging, available, responsive, empathic, reliable, soothing, compassionate, reassuring, supportive, sensitive, kind, caring, comforting, and accepting. Of course, many other secure characteristics exist, so feel free to expand the list.

Again, if you have survived your life so far, it is likely that you have received support and encouragement from someone, somewhere. These people could have been your primary caregiver, or they could have been a family member, friend, teacher, coach, mentor, therapist, or pet. You may also draw strength and guidance from a spiritual belief or a role model you admire. The possibilities for sources of support are endless.

Fortunately, I had many people who helped me survive my childhood traumas and reconnect me to my *Secure Self.* One of the most significant examples was my best friend and mentor, Lee, who personified these secure characteristics. During our conversations, I felt special and unique because she listened, understood, and accepted me just like I am. She reminded me of the goodness within me, even when I could not feel it. When I retreated under pressure, she encouraged me to move forward with a gentle and reassuring push. She helped me to open my heart and trust another human being with her reliability and love.

She made me a delicious vegetable soup when I was feeling sad and needed comfort. We would sit at her kitchen table, which always had fresh flowers from her lovely garden, and just talk. We shared personal stories and vulnerable truths that we feared others would judge if they discovered them. We continued connecting by sitting in front of the fireplace, tucking each other under the soft blankets as we sipped our tea.

We went to concerts and plays, had picnics, and went on long walks around beautiful places. We even flew a kite at the beach for fun, honoring our Inner Children who missed that opportunity growing up. We accepted each other's flaws and quirks, and if something bothered us, we trusted our relationship enough to address it directly. We cried, laughed, and created a strong bond by being ourselves while accepting and celebrating the other as she was.

The forty-year age difference in our friendship didn't matter. Lee was my mentor and friend on my journey (you can find pictures of us in the blog). She taught me what a secure relationship can be. We had such a deep bond, and I cherished her. Unfortunately, she passed away in 2018, just eight short weeks after her heart cancer diagnosis. I still deeply feel her with me and remember the quality of our unique relationship.

Can you recall some gems, like Lee, that helped you on your journey? If you can't remember any right now, that's perfectly fine. We will excavate more; I know they are there.

By the way, of course, there was a time in my life when you had asked me this exact question, and I would stare at you and give you the "What are you talking about?" look, and I would not be able to provide any names. But the deeper I dug into my healing journey, the more I realized how these gems that have come along carried me to the next step in my life without me even realizing it. For instance, my elementary school teacher, Şükran Hanım, in the small town we lived in, and my math teacher, Ertan Bey, when I was a teenager, were instrumental in my early life, as were many others who have supported me and will continue to do so.

Here is a brief visualization exercise that might be helpful. This practice can establish the groundwork for connecting to your *Secure Self*. You can access the visualization audio recording on the blog under the *Chapter 9* post (https://medium.com/@securechapters). After completing the exercise, feel free to write down your experience to reflect further.

Visualization Practice

Please take a comfortable position, either sitting or lying down. Now, close your eyes or point your gaze downward—whichever feels comfortable. Take some deep breaths and allow yourself to settle into your seat and come into your body, being present in the here and now.

Continue focusing on your breath and the sensations of your body's contact with your seat. Starting to embody the present moment. Inhale and exhale. Inhale and exhale.

Once you feel more grounded, I'd like you to think about a challenging time in your life when you received the support you needed. Think about someone or something that was there for you during that difficult time. Please try to choose someone you did not have a complicated relationship with. This relationship might even be a stranger who opened a door for you or someone special in your life who provided comfort at a dark time.

Now, take a moment to see that picture in your mind's eye. Start soaking in this loving, embracing, engaging, caring, and supportive relationship you had. It really doesn't matter how long it lasted.

Whether it was just a smile, a hug, a word, a look, an act of kindness, or whatever made you feel that you are not alone in this world, just feel that connection. Remember how you were cared for, even if just for a moment.

Imagine the sun warming you, the wind brushing through your hair, the earth supporting you, or a spiritual feeling that brings you security. You don't need to look too far. Just take a minute and allow your consciousness to rise.

It's also completely ok if nothing comes up. Just rest in the safety of your own breath for a moment.

Let your feelings soak in a bit more. Visualize your heart opening as feelings of warmth and support surround you. Allow yourself to be exactly where you are. Breathe in this connection and savor this moment. Take a couple more minutes to appreciate this meaningful connection. Inhaling and exhaling. And taking in the love.

And when you are ready, slowly open your eyes, returning to the here and now.

These moments that came up in your visualization are the gateways to your connection to your *Secure Self*. They provide clues about how your *Secure Self*'s guidance may feel. Unfortunately, some of us may not have had many secure external experiences, but this does not mean we cannot establish new inner and outer secure connections.

If Your Secure Self Guided Your Life, How Would It Be Different?

Why don't you give yourself a few minutes to imagine how you would approach life with your *Secure Self* guiding you? After you are done visualizing, take some time to write down what pops into your mind. Pay attention to what comes up when you think about your *Secure Self* being in the driver's seat of your life. What if that inner voice had the qualities of secure attachment?

When I ask myself this question, I visualize relating to the world more mindfully. I envision connecting with life in a softer and more trusting manner rooted deeply in love. I feel fierce and calm at the same time. I'm embodying this general sense of ease in approaching life and going with the flow of universal intelligence. When I find myself feeling scared or uncomfortable with doing something out of my comfort zone—like writing a book or trying something new like surfing or learning a new language—I can encourage myself to move forward. Throughout the day, I make it a habit to check in with myself to see how I feel or what I need. I trust my gut instincts and go with what feels like the flow of the moment. I am not trying to control life; instead, I am co-creating with it. I say yes to life and do not resist what's happening. I follow what feels good for my soul and do more of that. Whenever something challenging happens,

I soothe myself and move compassionately through my emotions. I have boundaries in place around people who do not bring love and peace into my life. I speak kindly to myself, get up, and try again after a failure. I like myself and all of my parts, and I know that I would swipe right for myself if I saw my profile on a dating app. I love who I am and am open to expanding that love. Most importantly, I feel safe and *Secure*.

Unfortunately, I'm not always in this *Secure* zone. Just like everyone else, I struggle with life's challenges. However, I am becoming better at recognizing when I'm out of flow and learning to be more compassionate towards myself while I work on getting back into the flow.

Throughout this journey, I have found some tools that have helped me build a stronger connection with my *Secure Self*. Now, let's explore what these tools are, shall we?

CHAPTER 10

Learned Optimism

After completing my undergraduate degree in psychology and working in the field for several years in Izmir, Türkiye, I decided to get my graduate degree to continue exploring the human psyche and learning to be more efficient in helping my clients.

After work, I started studying for the GRE and TOEFL exams and dreamed of getting accepted to graduate school. After many applications and grueling interviews in 2006, I got accepted to Purdue University Calumet's prestigious Marriage and Family Therapy (MFT) program. That August, I gathered all my courage for this new adventure and came to the United States to start my master's degree with my two luggage and without knowing anyone.

As one of the program requirements, the MFT graduate students (also called therapist interns) provided therapy services to clients at the Purdue Calumet Couple and Family Therapy Center while receiving intensive supervision from their experienced professors, who were approved by the American Association for Marriage and Family Therapy (AAMFT).

Because this center was a training facility, clients could receive affordable therapy sessions depending on their income. All clients had to be informed of all the requirements if they would like to receive services at this center. It was a great learning opportunity for graduate students and an excellent way to serve the community in Hammond, Indiana.

Every December, as the cohorts completed their year-long internships at the center, all clients were transferred to the new cohort of therapist interns. That year, in this transition process, one of the clients, Mary, specifically requested to be assigned to an older Christian male therapist intern. She stated that she was comfortable with and had built a great rapport with her current therapist intern, who had those characteristics and wanted to continue on that path with the new one.

Well, guess who got assigned to Mary? Yup, you're right. A Turkish woman of color therapist intern in her mid-twenties who speaks English as her second language and has just moved across the pond. What a plot twist!

All I can say is that this pairing was a fantastic experience for both of us. I will never forget Mary, my first client in the United States. Her goodbye gift from nearly two decades ago, with an inscription: "Wherever you go, go with your heart," a saying from Confucius, is still in my office and so dear to my heart.

Mary and I were pretty different on paper, yet we helped one another grow tremendously outside our comfort zones. When we first met, Mary had recently started therapy due to experiencing panic attacks at work. She was a single mother and a dedicated nurse with a fourteen-year-old son, who was her pride and joy. Our common sarcastic sense of humor helped us deal with me not being the older Christian male therapist intern.

As our therapist and client relationship grew over the months, I integrated my research project into our sessions (I know, shocker, right? #nerdalert). In real time, I enthusiastically shared what I found for my master's thesis. Luckily, Mary was open to learning and loved any research I integrated into our sessions.

One of the *Inner Security* tools we worked on was a concept called Learned Optimism[1], coined by Dr. Martin Seligman, a former president of the American Psychological Association and one of the founders of positive psychology. The field of positive psychology is the science of positive subjective experience, which focuses on well-being, contentment, satisfaction, hope, optimism, flow, and happiness[2]. If you remember, this field was introduced to me by Dr. Tedeschi a couple of years back with the post-traumatic growth concept.

Interestingly, before his work on Learned Optimism, Dr. Seligman was one of the originators of the Learned Helplessness theory[3], which influences how we look at clinical depression even today in the cognitive behavior therapy (CBT) field. Learned Helplessness theory asserts that due to experiencing unavoidable or uncontrollable situations, we may be conditioned not to respond to other problems even if we have some control over them. We might experience difficulty seeing different options or possibilities. Through these conditionings, we may feel helpless, stuck, and depressed. After spending several decades studying Learned Helplessness theory, Dr. Seligman turned to exploring the other side of the coin and asked: *If helplessness is learned, can optimism also be learned?*

When I came across his book, *Learned Optimism: How to Change Your Mind and Your Life*[1], I was just at the beginning of grad school, and I had no idea how it would help my clients and me. Okay, the behind-the-scenes story was actually a bit more personal. I was going through a gut-wrenching breakup (pretty typical in our twenties, right?) thousands of miles away from my home country, and I was looking for a research-based self-help book that could ease my tremendous suffering! I guess the saying when the student is ready, the teacher appears is true because the book showed up randomly in my life when I needed it the most.

After reading this book, I was excited about learning more about this concept and decided to study it for my master's thesis (#silverlining). There was only one barrier: persuading my thesis advisor to integrate the positive psychology field with the marriage and family therapy field, which had not been done before. Well, I was in the Model United Nations (MUN) debate club in high school, so I think you can guess the outcome :).

The ABC Model

Once I got the green light to start my research, I started sharing with Mary my passion for understanding how we make meaning in our lives. According to cognitive behavior theory, when an event occurs, we conceptualize the event with the filter of our beliefs, which then influences our emotions and behaviors. This process is known as the ABC model[4,5], initially formulated by Dr. Albert Ellis and then frequently utilized in the CBT field, which Dr. Aaron Beck founded[6].

We explored the ABC model in more detail in one of our sessions. I drew a triangle on the board and discussed how events, thoughts, and feelings are connected. Mary and I used examples from her life to discuss the theory and make it more relatable to her.

In this model, 'A' stands for adversity (events), such as a trigger at work; 'B' stands for beliefs (thoughts), such as Mary thinking she might lose control due to a panic attack, and 'C' refers to the consequences (emotions/body sensations/behaviors), such as the intense anxiety and increased heart rate she felt.

Mary and I examined her learned negative beliefs, which kept her restricted and prevented her from thriving. Identifying and acknowledging the 'B' (the beliefs) was crucial to begin this process. We discussed the typical cognitive distortions[7,8] that we often use, which are unhelpful thought patterns that are shortcuts in our understanding of the world and, more often than not, are inaccurate filters. Our Anxious and Avoidant Parts utilize these cognitive distortions frequently, so paying attention to these barriers to our *Inner Security* can be very beneficial.

I provided Mary with a list of common cognitive distortions from Dr. Beck, which you can easily find online, to exemplify how our thinking can get us into trouble[7,8]. Mary said that she had two favorite ones that she used quite often. The first was "mind reading," which involves predicting what the other person is thinking without evidence or confirmation. The second was "should statements," which she often used with herself and others. Unfortunately, this put tremendous pressure on herself and her relationships. You would have loved to see her face when I asked, "Did you should on yourself this week?" We couldn't stop laughing for a long time during that session.

Next, we focused on the 'C,' the consequences we experience due to our beliefs. Let's say a traffic jam was going on, which is the adversity 'A,' and for Mary, the 'B' could be anything from "How dumb am I for not leaving earlier?" or "I hate this, why do I live in a big city anyway?" to "Oh shit, I'll definitely be fired for this." Usually, the costs for these thoughts, the 'C,' were frustration, anger, disappointment, headaches, and sometimes even an anxiety attack.

We discussed in detail how the emotions manifested in the body as physical sensations and how we can welcome them to understand their messages as Rumi encourages us. These investigative ways of exploring the intricate patterns of relating to the world helped her to slow down the reactionary process. She recognized that with awareness, we could make different choices if we wished to do so. This is the key to moving from reacting to responding.

The ABCDE Model

Dr. Seligman expanded the original ABC model and added the 'D' and 'E' when teaching optimism[1]. 'D' stands for disputation, the process of looking for evidence for our beliefs, exploring alternative ways to view the adversities in our lives, and reframing the situations. 'E' stands for energization, which occurs naturally after disputing the limiting beliefs.

For instance, in the traffic jam example, 'D' might sound like, "This traffic jam is not in my control; I don't even know what happened. All I can control right now is how I respond. I can calm myself down first and then tell the office what's happening. Let me see what can help at this moment. And in the future, I will check the road for traffic jams beforehand and leave a bit earlier to make sure." Then, her 'E' was experiencing more calmness in her body and feeling more regulated.

The effect of relating to ourselves more objectively, kinder, and compassionately was a game changer for her. We continued discussing different incidents in her life and examined the ABCDEs in each situation, which led Mary to recognize the 'E' more clearly after each investigation. She gained a deeper understanding of how our thoughts, feelings, body sensations, and behaviors are intertwined. She practiced relating to them more constructively and felt more optimistic.

"Now I get what goes on in my head more clearly, but how do I move forward? What do I do so these beliefs do not limit me? How do I dispute them effectively?" Mary asked. I was thrilled that she was genuinely interested in the following steps. "Well, we're going to explore the three **P**s," I replied. "Three what?" she asked, intrigued.

Three Ps

The "Three **P**s..." I continued to explain with excitement (Can you tell I love research?), "...are **P**ermanence, **P**ersonalization, and **P**ervasiveness, which refer to the quality of the beliefs we attribute to events[1]."

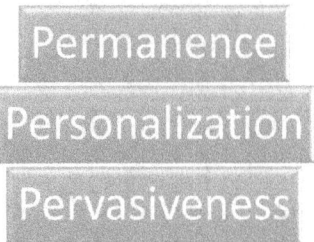

"The first **P** stands for permanence," I started explaining this model. "When we experience an event, especially one we perceive to be negative, we think that this event is going to last forever, right? She nodded her head. "What pops into your mind as I say that?" I asked.

"Well, when I experience a panic attack, and I am right in the middle of it, I feel I'm stuck, I can't breathe, I feel like I'm going to die, and it will never end," she replied.

Mary was describing her Anxious Part fully taking charge of her life at those moments. "That's a very clear way of explaining what permanence can feel like," I said. "When this happens, we can remind ourselves that this is a temporary situation and will not last forever. It will suck for a while, and it will end," I added. This can help us shift the focus to what can be done at the moment to alleviate the suffering.

"In these moments, not only do we think that the setback we are going through is permanent, but we also often think it is personal, which is the second **P**...Personalization. This **P** presents itself when you might be thinking, 'I'm the only one experiencing this,' or 'It is all because of me,' 'It is my fault,' or 'I caused this,'" I continued.

"Yeah, I'm a pretty good expert on that one, too," Mary said, smiling. I loved the playfulness in our sessions.

"The questions we can ask ourselves to identify the personalization aspect may be: Is this all about me, or are other circumstances contributing to it? Is this about my personality or the effort that I put into it? Am I personally responsible, or are there other external influences beyond my control?

Here, we are looking for a more objective way to explain the causes of the events. Think about it like a pie chart with multiple reasons for that particular event. This might help you identify different possibilities. If you are blowing a red light, it's easy; that was a personal decision. Then, we need to take accountability," I explained.

Mary jumped in and said, "I was just going to ask you about that because I feel like this might sound like a bit of a justification for not owning up to our wrongdoings and finding excuses."

We were so in sync that I explained to her how part of this **P** bothered me until I read about Dr. Seligman's suggestion of exploring each event individually, definitely taking responsibility when needed, and not generalizing that we are responsible for everything[1]. He further underlined that the mindset of Personalization can be very destructive, especially when people feel depressed and already internalize all the negativity around them. This is why we need to be extra careful at those times.

"Assigning causes appropriately and looking at the situation objectively is essential for disputing cognitive distortions. We are not the reason for everything that happens to us, and it's important to discern that," I continued.

Mary nodded and said, "Yeah, that's so true. When I am feeling down, I carry the whole weight of the world, so it might be good to let some of the shit go."

"Tell me about the last **P**," Mary asked.

"The last **P** is for pervasiveness," I replied. "You see, when we experience something unpleasant, whether an emotion, a thought, or an event, we might feel that it impacts our entire life. Let's say we might be going through a break-up; we might still have a good family, a profession we like, hobbies, many close friends, and other positive aspects in our lives. It is a specific problem, not a pervasive one. Experiencing a challenging emotion or a thought is only part of our life, not the whole."

"I see what you mean," she said. "When I feel anxiety deeply, I can't think of anything positive in my life; the problem at hand becomes such a big deal, and my whole life becomes unmanageable."

"Yes, that is very common for most of us," I replied. "Furthermore, research shows that if individuals facing challenging situations ask the questions: 'Is this permanent, is this personal, and is this pervasive?' and answer 'yes' to all three, they tend to have a more depressive attributional style. And if they say 'no' to these **Ps**, they have more of an optimistic attributional style[3]. Again, I would like to consider this a spectrum, not a dichotomy," I said.

"One way of practicing optimism is by asking these **3Ps** to ourselves and allowing ourselves to put things into perspective by soothing our brain that is an expert on creating these Oscar-worthy catastrophic movie scripts," I added.

"Wow!" she said. "That makes so much sense." Through this exploration, Mary slowly realized she had different options for responding to challenging life experiences and could bounce back. I love seeing this shift in my clients.

When Mary came to the therapy room for the next session, she immediately took something out of her purse. This was not very common as we tended to take care of payment and scheduling at the end of the session, so I was curious. "Look what I have done!" She pulled a notecard from her wallet. "What is that?" I asked. Mary had a big, proud grin on her face.

"These are the three questions that we discussed for the **3Ps**. I wrote them on a notecard, and of course, I had to bedazzle it a bit," she smiled. She had decorated the card, and it looked great. "I started carrying this notecard with me, and when I felt like my lid would blow off, I took it out and asked the three questions about the setback I was experiencing. 'Is this permanent? Is this personal? Is this pervasive?' I can't describe how much this tool has already helped me. I don't feel like I will lose it as quickly anymore, and it allowed me to respond to my son more calmly. I also repeated to myself: 'Not permanent, not personal, not pervasive,' like a mantra," she said. I absolutely loved what she did and how she created resiliency. In these moments, I have so much gratitude for my profession.

Mary liked observing the processes in her mind as if we were watching a slow-motion movie. She appreciated figuring out some of the underlying mechanisms of our inner workings. She loved the phrase I often used, which I learned early in my career: *Don't believe everything you think.* This was a way of creating a healthy distance from our thoughts and not identifying with them. Observing our thoughts without going along with the storyline empowered Mary and gave her hope for self-regulation, which is a significant part of strengthening our *Inner Security.*

During our last sessions, I presented Mary with the findings of my master's thesis. The data I gathered confirmed that individuals who scored **higher** in:

a. **differentiation** (the ability to distinguish between emotions and thoughts & being able to form intimate relationships that are both connected and interdependent),

b. **family coping** (strategies for managing emotional distress), and

c. **family functioning** (problem-solving skills and communication patterns)

were more likely to have a positive outlook and **higher levels of optimism**[9]. This was the first study in the marriage and family therapy field, combining positive psychology principles and providing tools for building strengths in individuals and families.

A decade later than these conversations with Mary, I heard Sheryl Sandberg, a previous high-ranking executive, giving a commencement keynote speech at the University of California (UC) Berkeley about how she used the **3Ps** in her healing journey to cope with her husband's sudden death. You can find her speech on YouTube[10].

Shortly after that powerful speech, in 2017, she released a New York Times bestseller book, Option B[11], which she wrote with her friend and psychologist, Adam Grant, discussing loss, the **3Ps,** and resiliency. She also founded OptionB.Org, which has many valuable resources to help us with life's hardships. What a beautiful way research can help us get out of the hole, support us, and improve our well-being.

CHAPTER 11

———— ❧ ————

Self-Compassion

In the fall of 2009, I began my doctoral studies at Purdue University, and this time, I moved to Lafayette, Indiana. It had been a couple of years since I arrived from Türkiye for graduate school, and I was still trying to figure things out as an international student while adjusting to a new culture. Although the transition was difficult, I was incredibly grateful that I could be able to work and put myself through school. I rented a charming one-bedroom apartment on the lovely Ferry Street and later adopted Lily, my beloved dog.

These life changes led me to search for a therapist to help deal with my fears, concerns, and the overwhelming stress of going through a doctorate program. I knew that to be an effective therapist, I needed to unpack my emotional baggage, which was a big one. Therefore, I started a search for a therapist who was a good match for me.

This meant finding someone trained in systemic thinking and with extensive clinical experience. I also preferred to work with someone with first-hand knowledge of the challenges of attending a demanding Ph.D. program. That was a tall order, but after researching and talking to other graduate students, I found a therapist who was a former Purdue graduate. I was excited and nervous to start this healing journey with him.

I wanted to share this story to encourage you to find the right therapist if you're considering therapy. The relationship between a therapist and their client is the most critical aspect of the psychotherapy process. Research conducted by my late professor, Dr. Douglas Sprenkle, and his colleagues on common factors supports this point[1]. Therefore, it may be helpful to talk to multiple therapists to see how they connect with you and trust your intuition to decide which is best for you. Remember, dear one, you are the expert in your life and will know what is a good fit.

As expected, my therapy opened Pandora's box and revealed many memories that needed to be processed. Meanwhile, I was trying to complete my doctoral studies and navigate the politics of academia. A lot was going on all at once, and I was struggling.

Finding Self-Compassion

In one of our sessions, my therapist introduced a new concept to help me cope with my challenges: *self-compassion.* I was intrigued as I had never heard about it before, and since then, as a recovering perfectionist, self-compassion has helped me stay emotionally sober. A gentler way of relating to myself when I am in pain was an incredible gift from my therapist that I really needed, and now it is my pleasure to share this *Inner Security* tool with you.

A decade later, self-compassion remained an integral part of my life. This time, I was working as an assistant professor in the Purdue University Northwest MFT program and serving as the interim clinic director in the Purdue University Northwest Couple and Family Therapy Center. It was a full circle moment for me, returning to where I started in the United States.

After seeing the benefits of self-compassion in my own life and the lives of my clients, I integrated self-compassion research into the curriculum for all of the classes I taught at Purdue. This was a brand-new approach in this graduate program, and I knew exploring it would be worthwhile. At the beginning of the semester, I asked my students to take the self-compassion questionnaire at https://self-compassion.org/self-compassion-test/ and then retake it and compare their scores at the end of the semester after the work we did in class (feel free to take it yourself with the link provided). My intention was for them first to experience the benefits of self-compassion practices and then introduce the skills to their clients.

While teaching the trauma class, I received valuable feedback from my graduate students regarding incorporating self-compassion in trauma work in their sessions. They noted that it had a very positive impact on their clients. (I truly miss you all! Good beans! Don't worry, this is not a typo; it's just an inside joke after my students taught me the phrase 'cool beans,' and I kept mistakenly saying good beans, which cracked them up!)

Some of my students were so interested in the self-compassion research that they chose to study it further for their master's thesis and asked me to be their thesis advisor. I could not begin to express how ecstatic all of these made me. Witnessing the ripple effect was amazing. I loved passing on the torch of helping others that was given to me by my mentors and seeing how my students were also doing the same with their clients and their research.

Okay, after all of these commercials, it's now time to explore self-compassion on a deeper level and see why it is vital for our mental health. Let's get some coffee (or your favorite beverage) and first dig into the research aspect. Then, we can look at the process in the clinical practice with the help of my client, Mindy. How does that sound?

Research on Self-Compassion

In 2003, Dr. Kristin Neff introduced the first research articles on self-compassion[2,3]. She borrowed the concept from Buddhism and brought it into the psychology field to be researched. Dr. Neff created a scale that allowed other researchers to explore this topic further. Her excellent book, *Self-Compassion: The Proven Power of Being Kind to Yourself*, provides valuable information and offers many practices[4].

For me, the best explanation of self-compassion came from Dr. Kristen Neff when I attended a training in March 2019 given by her and Dr. Christopher Germer in Reisterstown, Maryland. I remember tearing up when Dr. Neff said, "Self-compassion is a way of caring for ourselves as we would care for someone we truly love."

With self-compassion, we create an opening to connect to ourselves with a kinder inner voice. We learn to be our own best friend, our own support person, and our own ally, which is a very worthwhile journey to embark upon. However, this is not an easy task for most of us. Unfortunately, without intervention, our critical inner voice (the old radio station) is often fueled by our families and society's unrealistic expectations, comparisons, and pressures.

Most of us have been taught that the harder we are on ourselves, the better we will perform. Inevitably, we internalize these critical messages from outside, leading to self-abuse. Research indicates that 78% of us treat ourselves worse than we treat others[5]. Isn't it interesting how we readily show compassion to others but are not as quick to give it to ourselves?

Practicing self-compassion is like learning a new language filled with love, understanding, patience, encouragement, respect, and love. Instead of being judgmental of ourselves, which is ineffective in achieving goals, we can motivate and support ourselves with a self-compassionate voice, the new radio station that we can tune in and listen to.

Self-compassionate people rebound from adversity faster because it is easier to get up and try again with an encouraging, coach-like inner voice. Research has shown that self-compassion has significant correlations with post-traumatic stress recovery[6]. Moreover, self-compassion is becoming a crucial part of military mental health because of this bouncing-back effect. In one study, researchers found self-compassion to be a predictor of PTSD symptoms among Iraq and Afghanistan war veterans[7]. In my practice, these studies have helped me persuade my police officers and veteran clients about practicing self-compassion as a way to prevent developing trauma symptoms.

Mindy was one of my clients with whom I put self-compassion at the center of our work. She was in her early 20s and had recently begun her gender transition journey. Mindy came to me for help with anxiety and depression. These symptoms are found to be more common in the transgender population than in the cis population[8,9], and extra help and support are critical.

Mindy faced a difficult situation with her family, who did not fully accept her identity as a transgender individual. Despite Mindy's efforts to communicate her preferred pronouns and name, her parents did not respect her wishes, and their personal beliefs prevented them from supporting Mindy's transition.

As a highly creative individual, Mindy was pursuing her dream of becoming a graphic designer. Fortunately, her friend network provided her with vital support at this time of her life. She also utilized other resources such as The Trevor Project and GLAAD. I admired her strength and felt honored to be alongside her.

"Am I going to just sit on my couch, eat chocolate chip ice cream while watching Netflix all day long, and give up on my dreams if I'm being self-compassionate?" she asked.

"Well, that's a very specific visual right there, Mindy," I smiled and said. "Not that there's anything wrong with binge-watching shows with eating ice cream sometimes (been there and done that!), but are you worried that being kind to yourself will make you lose motivation? Did I understand you correctly?" She nodded in agreement. This was a common concern expressed by many of my clients when I introduced the concept of self-compassion.

"I was curious about the same thing," I said. "After some research, I discovered that many studies have shown that practicing self-compassion leads to higher motivation[10], post-traumatic growth[11], goal achievement[12], happiness[13], and grit[14]. It has also been proven to reduce anxiety, depression, suicidal ideation, and perfectionism[15, 16,17,18]. Would you like to learn more about self-compassion and maybe even try some exercises together?"

"Well, I guess I wouldn't mind being happier, so let's just do it," she replied.

CHAPTER 12

———⚮———

Practicing
Self-Compassion

During our next meeting, Mindy was eager to learn more about self-compassion. She was always attentive and engaged in the nerdy TED talks I gave during our sessions. She asked great questions and successfully applied the information to her daily life. It was an absolute pleasure to work with her.

"Self-compassion has three main elements: *mindfulness, common humanity,* **and** *self-kindness*[1,2]. We can think about them as the legs of a stool; all are essential. These three components help us learn how to treat ourselves with compassion. However, developing these new neural pathways may take some time, like any other skill. So, there are no microwave answers," I explained. She responded with a sarcastic "ha ha, very funny" look while squeezing her eyes.

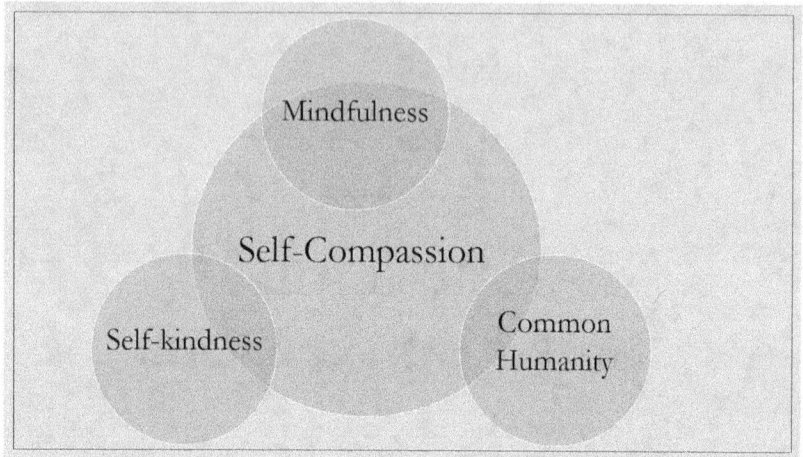

"The first component, *mindfulness*, is all about noticing what is happening with ourselves, especially during times of pain and suffering. It is the opposite of over-identifying with what we are experiencing," I continued to explain. "We are not our feelings, thoughts, or problems; we are so much more than that. We are the consciousness observing these experiences happening to us.

When we're on autopilot, we often react to situations so quickly that we're unaware of our feelings, thoughts, and why we're reacting the way we are. But if we're mindful, we can pause and take note of the fact that we might be in pain. We can then say to ourselves, 'I'm struggling,' 'I'm in pain,' or 'I feel really bad right now.'

We can progress towards healing and growth by acknowledging what's happening within ourselves instead of minimizing, avoiding, over-identifying, gaslighting, or dismissing it," I continued. Mindy looked interested as she sipped her matcha latte and listened to my pitch about self-compassion. I felt like I was in the show Shark Tank[3], trying to promote a revolutionary product for the betterment of humankind.

"The second component is **common humanity**, which means that we are all connected, we all suffer, and we all try to go through the world as best we can. If you think about it, thousands, if not millions, of people may be feeling what we are feeling at the same time," I explained.

"This is the opposite of isolation. We are not alone in our human experiences. Pain is a part of life, and it's impossible to avoid it completely. I guess only psychopaths might not feel it much," I continued as Mindy smiled.

"Everyone feels shitty sometimes. After acknowledging the pain, we can remind ourselves that we are not alone. We can say to ourselves, 'Pain is a part of life,' 'Life is full of shit,' 'Suffering is a human experience,' 'Everyone suffers,' 'We are all in the same boat,' or 'I'm holding hands with millions of people on the planet feeling just like me right now,'" I concluded.

"I don't get it completely. How does realizing that we are in a shit show helpful for us?" Mindy asked.

I appreciated her cutting-to-the-chase attitude. "Well, because it's not only about the shit show," I said, "it's about realizing that you're not alone in the shit show."

"It's humbling to realize that the pain we feel, which seems excruciating and unique, is not uncommon. We are all on this planet, riding through the trillions of galaxies. The angst, the zest, and anything in between that we experience are also felt by others. We are all connected and not alone," I added.

This awareness did not come to me quickly. I still remember feeling incredibly lonely and sad during one of the self-compassion meditations Dr. Neff led. I didn't know anyone in the conference hall who had traveled from different countries to attend this unique training. To be honest, I was skeptical about how putting my hand on my heart would erase the pain I felt. But I decided to give it a try, and something miraculous happened.

As tears streamed down my face, a visual of a world map appeared in my mind. I saw the images of the participants from the conference hall appearing from different parts of the world and telling me I was not alone and that I belonged. My heart melted.

There was nothing wrong with me; I was hurting a lot, and I needed support. That training changed me and my life. I was introduced to many amazing people all around the world. I even met one of my best friends from Costa Rica there. Who could have predicted that years later, I would visit her and live in her amazing country for several months? But that's a story for another book.

"The last component, *self-kindness*, is about how we can gently respond to ourselves with compassion while facing life's inevitable difficulties. This is the opposite of self-judgment, where we often ask ourselves, 'Why am I feeling this way? It shouldn't be this way. There is something wrong with me.'

"With self-compassion, we focus on comforting ourselves as we would comfort a close friend who is going through a tough time. For most of us, this capacity comes naturally, right? Immediately, we can support them, ask them what they need, and be there for them. I remember Mindy, you were telling me that your friends come to you for emotional support often, right? That sounds like you are a compassionate friend," I said. She blushed.

"With self-kindness, we do the same for ourselves. We can, for instance, ask ourselves: What do I need right now? How can I be kind to myself today? What can make me feel a little better right now?" I continued.

Mindy looked at me and added, "Or, in other words: 'This is a shit show. I'm not alone in this shit show. How can I feel less shitty right now?'"

I loved her sense of humor. "That's exactly what I'm talking about. I'll make sure I explain this concept like this to my future clients from now on," I replied.

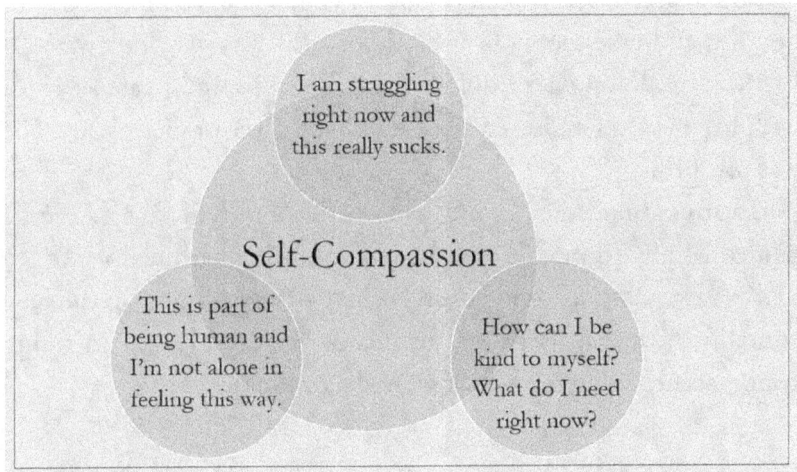

Mindy found the aspect of self-compassion that involves non-attachment to our thoughts and feelings very useful. When she experienced panic attacks, she benefited from observing her experience without identifying with the panic.

She validated herself and acknowledged that having a panic attack was difficult while also remembering that it was temporary (I had taught her the 3Ps previously). Mindy also reminded herself that many others experience panic attacks and that she was not alone. She then asked herself what could help calm her nervous system and began to show kindness to herself. In doing so, she was learning to become her own ally. This is how having *Inner Security* looks in action.

Mindy and I continued to talk about how when we are feeling shitty, we can take a few minutes to remind ourselves of the three parts of self-compassion. Choosing sentences from each component that resonate with us can help us lift ourselves up, just like a supportive friend would.

You can also remind yourself of these components like your own mantras, carry them on a note card in your wallet as Mary did with her 3Ps, and take them out in times of a shit show. Mindy was also very creative. Using her graphic design strengths, she created a visual with her mantras and used it as her screen saver on her phone. She was just brilliant.

To strengthen this process, at the end of one of our sessions, I guided Mindy through a practice of connecting with her *Secure Self* and experiencing self-compassion. The *Chapter 12* post on the blog contains the audio recording for this meditation (https://medium. com/@securechapters). Would you like to join us?

Self-Compassion Meditation

Please sit or lie down in a position you feel most comfortable. We are showing up for ourselves today. Remember, we are letting the outside world be outside of us, creating this inner container and connecting to ourselves on a deeper level. This is such a needed time for all of us in this chaotic world.

Now, close your eyes or lower your gaze to the floor, whichever you prefer, that will make you feel the safest. Please slowly bring your attention to your breath. Focus on your breathing pattern and see if you can slow it down a bit. Inhaling and exhaling.

While slowly inhaling and exhaling, marvel at what your body is doing with this oxygen. How it just knows what to do with that breath of fresh air. Imagine how the oxygen travels in your blood all the way to each cell in your body.

Soak in this extraordinary process and how you are part of this extraordinary life. How you are connected to everything and how you are part of everything.

Now, try to connect to your Secure Self, which has unconditional love and acceptance for you. Your Secure Self cherishes who you are and is proud of who you are becoming. Your Secure Self is the observer within you and connected to the whole universe.

If you have difficulty connecting with your Secure Self, consider one of your favorite childhood memories. Remember that you were born with security. You were born with trust. You were born with love. You were Secure. You were connected to the universe. You arrived here for a reason.

And remember that this loving, Secure Self has always been there. It might have just been hard to feel it. And that's ok. You now remember that it has been with you throughout your life. You are loved, and you are worthy.

If it is still hard for you to connect, ask for directions to connect to your Secure Self. Let go of thinking and feel the senses throughout your body, your breathing. Focus on just being, not doing.

Now, recall a recent experience that was somewhat painful to you. Because we are just learning this new skill of self-compassion, please choose an experience that is not too powerful on your nervous system. Maybe on a scale of 0-10 of a disturbance level, at most a 2 or a 3 as we start.

Now, bring up the mindfulness component of self-compassion and use the first part of your mantra. Validate your experience and allow it to take space in your life as it is here. Please take a couple of deep breaths and let it all sink in.

Then connect to the other human beings in the world who might be feeling this type of discomfort and put your hand on their hearts. Tell them they are not alone. Then, put your hand on your heart and tell yourself that you are also not alone.

And finally, see if there is any message that this discomfort has to tell you. See if it wants you to accept the inevitable, take some action, voice something, or do anything else it needs from you to feel honored finally.

Now, let the Secure Self speak to you. Just listen. This might take a minute, but it will arrive. Let your Secure Self provide what the discomfort needs from you. Let your Secure Self lovingly soothe you. Feel what Inner Security feels like.

Experience this Inner Security as a gift only you can give to yourself whenever needed. A security that you can tap into when you need support. A security that comes from deep inner knowing of yourself. Just open your heart and let the love in. Trust and you will receive.

Trust this Secure Self that is connected to all others' Secure Selves. Trust this part that is connected to universal intelligence. Trust the interconnectedness. Trust the process of finding true love within yourself, those around you, and the whole universe.

Ask for guidance if you need help from your Secure Self. Ask for the recipe if you are hungry for self-love. Let the loving words you need appear in your mind. Let the loving images guide you. Let your inner knowing help you. Trust and you will receive. Feel relief in knowing the answers are in you. Feel the soothing comfort that is always within you.

Now, slowly focus your attention back on your breathing. Inhale and exhale. Feel your body's sensations. Then, gently come back to the here and now.

Please open your eyes and welcome the present, dear one.

CHAPTER 13

Secure Base and
Safe Haven

The love and care we receive in our early years significantly influence our worldview. According to Dr. Bowlby, when we have attachment figures who are responsive, supportive, and nurturing towards us in childhood, they become our secure base and safe haven[1,2].

During childhood, having a **Secure Base** gives us the confidence to explore the world, try new things, and discover our likes and dislikes. This is the first pillar of attachment security, which is crucial for our emotional and psychological development. When we feel that we've been allowed to go out, grow, and experience this amazing life, we also learn that we can always return to a secure space whenever we need a little reassurance.

If our caregivers were our secure base during childhood, they would have encouraged us to be our best selves and celebrated our successes with us. They would have helped us identify our strengths to reach our full potential. By being our secure base, they teach us to trust ourselves and eventually become our own secure base.

The **Safe Haven** concept, the second pillar of attachment security, means that we can trust our caregivers and depend on them for comfort and care when needed. Deep down, don't we all need someone to acknowledge our pain and help us work through it? Don't we all need support and comfort when life gets tough?

Through sensitive and secure attachment modeling, we experience being comforted and soothed by our attachment figures. Gradually, this co-regulation transforms into self-regulation. However, if there are injuries in attachment security, such as inattentiveness, unresponsiveness, inconsistencies, gaslighting, or invalidation, we might struggle with self-regulation and being our own safe haven.

Having a secure base and safe haven is comforting, but not everyone gets to experience that with their caregivers. However, this doesn't preclude us from creating new neural pathways and experiencing *Inner Security*. As adults, it is possible for us to cultivate reliance on our *Secure Self* as our internal secure base and safe haven.

Our *Secure Self* can compassionately guide us on our healing journey and become a source of comfort and support during challenging times. Like a best friend, our *Secure Self* can encourage and motivate us to explore life to the fullest. By developing trust in ourselves, we can emerge as our own allies, providing the support we deserve. When in need of inspiration, we can imagine the way Jonathan Van Ness from *Queer Eye* expresses care and love (saying *Yas Queen!*), which always warms my heart and brings a big smile.

Dear one, we are all in this together. Even though we are unique in many ways, we are similar in many others. All of us desire to be loved, seen and heard. We want to be celebrated for who we are, and we want to heal. The cool thing is that now we can do this together. You are not alone. (Note: Please play the *This is Me³* song from The Greatest Showman for an emotional effect! Thank you for listening ;).)

Healing the Inner Child by Becoming Our Own Secure Base and Safe Haven

A significant part of my healing journey involved learning how to allow my *Secure Self* to care for the younger part of me, my Inner Child. This term was first introduced to me by my therapist when we were talking about how I felt when I was a kid, which opened the door for me to start getting to know my Inner Child and her unmet needs.

Compassionately reparenting our Inner Child involves creating a secure base and a safe haven within ourselves. Reparenting is the process of securely responding to our Inner Child. In this practice, we prioritize our Inner Child, notice their needs, and meet them with our *Secure Self.* Inner Child healing is all about trust and consistency. With our consistent actions, the Inner Child gradually begins to feel that the *Secure Self* is taking care of them, allowing them to be who they want to be.

Reparenting can begin to be established by a psychological concept called mirroring. When someone mirrors us, we feel seen and heard and understand that our emotions are valid. We get the message that there's nothing wrong with feeling that way, and emotions can be sorted out, and eventually, they will pass. Our emotions will move through us like clouds in the sky or a leaf strolling a river. We can see them, be with them, honor them, and let them go lovingly, just like Rumi says.

To understand how important mirroring is in a baby's life, please search online for the "Still Face Experiment" video by Dr.

Edward Tronick[4]. This experiment was carried out at a university research laboratory, and it shows the baby's heartbreaking response when his mother stops responding to him. Even a brief period of unresponsiveness can have a significant impact on the baby, so imagine the consequences of prolonged unresponsiveness.

Attachment injuries, which refer to the lack of emotional attentiveness and responsiveness, can cause wounds in our early development. When these injuries are repeated and left unaddressed, the Anxious and Avoidant Parts are formed. Therefore, giving ourselves unconditional love, acceptance, and mirroring is crucial when communicating with our Inner Child and allowing our parts to heal.

First, we see ourselves and validate our own experience compassionately, regardless of what it is and how it feels. Once we understand and support that Inner Child, they will start feeling calmer and trusting us more. We will then allow our *Secure Self* to reparent and become the secure base and safe haven we need for ourselves.

A supportive and encouraging inner voice that acknowledges your feelings and empathizes with you can make your Inner Child feel seen, heard, and relaxed. Sentences like "That sounds pretty tough," "I can understand how you feel," "I would be so frustrated if I were in your shoes too," "I'm so sorry. This is very sad," "It makes sense why you feel this way," "I'm so proud of you," or "I'm here for you" can lead to deeper connections with your Inner Child and start providing the reparenting that they need.

Now, let's have some fun and explore becoming a **secure base** for ourselves. I invite you to think about what made you happy as a kid and create a list of those things. I still remember the joy I felt climbing onto the mulberry trees at my grandparents' house in Cunda Island. Though I may not be making that climb anytime soon, writing it down gave me a moment of happiness. Please take a couple of minutes to reflect on this. You can also expand that list by adding new things your Inner Child might want to try now. Creativity makes us happy. So why don't we get creative and enjoy the process?

Inner Child Happiness List

*	*
*	*
*	*
*	*
*	*
*	*
*	*
*	*

The next step is to incorporate the activities that bring joy into your life now. You can take the next few weeks to see how it feels to do the things from your list. When you actively try something from the list, consider what being a secure base means for you and focus on encouraging freedom, expression, exploration, and play. Relating to your Inner Child in a secure way from your *Secure Self* may be a new experience for you, and it may require practice.

While completing this exercise, consider taking out a picture of yourself when you were younger and look at how adorable you were. Keep this picture in mind when you're reparenting your Inner Child and when you're doing activities together. You can carry this picture in your wallet or make it a screensaver on your phone. You are so worthy and lovable. Now, it's time to give this special one the attention and affection they deserve from your *Secure Self*.

Here are some of the items I've tried with my Inner Child, and I hope they inspire you:

Hiking, going to children's movies, journaling with my non-dominant hand, zorbing (rolling inside a massive plastic ball), trying karate, running with a kite at the beach, swimming, cooking class, beach yoga, surfing, climbing El Penon, watching sea turtles when they are born, snorkeling, biking, mandala making, painting, reading cartoons, making vision boards, indoor rock climbing, ziplining, riding recumbent bicycle, river rafting, hot air balloon ride, running with my dog on the beach, parasailing, computer animation class, Zumba, Salsa, visiting the zoo, sewing, Ebru making, kayaking, eating sunflower seeds, paddleboarding, visiting new cities/countries, playing ultimate frisbee, napping, dipping cookies in tea as I did with my grandma, whale watching, dancing, reading Pippi Longstocking as I did when I was a kid, staying at a llama farm, taking road trips, and going to breakfast/lunch/dinner dates by myself.

During each of these reparenting trials, I had the intention in mind that I was doing things for my Inner Child and with my Inner Child. Spending time with yourself is crucial in discovering what makes you happy. The main idea is to get to know yourself better by trying new things and finding joy in them. Remember, there is no timeline for this process. You are building a lifelong, *Secure* relationship with yourself and becoming your own secure base.

As our Inner Child receives healthy reparenting from our *Secure Self*, we will naturally feel the desire for more exploration and play because we now have a secure base. The curiosity and joy of life will gradually emerge. This exploration is where the foundation of our interpersonal skills is slowly formed. Children are curious and progressively develop more verbal skills, which enable them to ask questions and try to understand how the world works. A child can grow creatively if curiosity is encouraged and celebrated.

With the support of play and curiosity, the seeds of purpose are also planted. As we pay attention to our Inner Child and form this secure inner attachment, we will meet others on the journey and form our tribe. We will welcome new experiences, people, and places into our lives. We will live more authentically and vibrantly.

CHAPTER 14

---⚭---

Reparenting

In the journey towards healing from attachment injuries endured in earlier life stages, our brains need secure corrective experiences to create new neural pathways. Therefore, prioritizing the cultivation of self-regulation skills becomes crucial in the process of reparenting our Inner Child. While this might initially sound daunting, the good news is that our *Secure Self* can now provide the co-regulation skills missing from childhood and proceed with forming the novel brain circuitry. To tailor this unique inner support effectively, let's engage in collecting some pertinent data, shall we?

Consider this: if you currently have a young child at home, take some time to think about what helps to calm them down. These may include soothing words, gentle touch, or a reassuring look. If you don't have a child, reflect on your most positive childhood memories, particularly instances when you felt well-supported. And if you didn't have many positive experiences growing up, try to remember a caring interaction you observed in another way, whether through relatives, teachers, friends, books, TV, or other means. Please take a few moments for this reflection, as we will revisit and build upon it shortly.

Through the practice of reparenting our Inner Child, we will discover how to become a **safe haven** for ourselves. In this transformative process, we may benefit from incorporating various self-soothing techniques that I often teach my clients for their *Inner Security Toolbox*.

Let's begin with one of the quickest and simplest ways to regulate our nervous system. Emotional pain often triggers shallow chest breathing and a flood of worst-case scenarios. In these moments, shifting to diaphragmatic breathing and slowing down exhalation can activate our parasympathetic nervous system[1]. This signals our amygdala that we are not in immediate danger (there are no tigers chasing us!), allowing us to calm ourselves and tap into our *Inner Security*.

A specific evidence-based tool for this purpose is the 4-7-8 breathing technique, frequently practiced in my therapy sessions[2]. To try it yourself, inhale for four seconds, hold for seven, and exhale for eight as if exhaling through a straw. Repeat this cycle about four times to experience a noticeable decrease in heart rate. This technique effectively activates the vagus nerve, promoting a calmer state.

Another technique I often introduce to my clients is the butterfly hug, utilized in EMDR. This method entails embracing oneself in a hug and tapping alternate shoulders during moments of stress, stimulating both sides of the brain and fostering a calmer nervous system. Combining this technique with diaphragmatic breathing enhances its effectiveness.

Listening to bilateral music also engages both brain hemispheres, providing soothing relief for an activated nervous system. You can easily find numerous soundtracks labeled "bilateral" or binaural" online and see how you like them. Personally, when feeling overwhelmed, I often put on one of these tracks and go for a walk. The combination of bilateral sounds and bilateral movement accelerates the calming of my limbic system, leaving me feeling significantly better afterward.

During one of my therapy sessions, I was struggling with keeping myself grounded. That's when my therapist shared with me the 5-4-3-2-1 technique. He encouraged me to look around and name five things I could see, four things I could touch, three things I could hear, two things I could smell, and one thing I could taste. After doing this exercise, I felt more present in the room, and my anxiety reduced significantly. I learned firsthand how this technique can help redirect focus to the present moment, aligning the mind and body.

Additionally, there is growing evidence supporting the efficacy of the Emotional Freedom Technique (EFT). This involves tapping the body's meridian points while discussing emotions and desired outcomes, which has been proven to calm anxiety and reduce heart rate[3]. I find practicing this technique with my clients very helpful in welcoming all their emotions and experiences. Many resources for exploring this technique can be found online.

Remember, dear one, these are different ways to self-support and self-love. By learning various tools, we can have more options to choose from when experiencing unpleasant emotions. Not every *Inner Security* tool always works, and some only work occasionally. Depending on our level of nervous system activation, different tools may be more effective at different times. By becoming more self-attuned, we will be better equipped to calm our nervous system using the most effective technique for that moment.

In therapy, I often explain this to my clients using the combination of the traffic light and the hand metaphor we discussed earlier. Feeling relaxed and safe makes responding to life more effortless. When our lid is secure, we are connected and grounded. This is the green zone, where we feel safe and relaxed. Life is manageable in this space as we can access our higher-level cognitive skills and regulate our emotions.

As our stress intensifies, entering the yellow zone, our emotional state may shift to discomfort, irritation, overwhelm, or agitation, causing our lid to loosen. In this phase, some cognitive abilities may still be accessible. If we recognize our activation early, we can take a detour before progressing into the red zone.

Once our lid is completely flipped, we are in the red zone and react to life more from our limbic system than our pre-frontal cortex. Actually, in the red zone, our prefrontal cortex is metaphorically offline. It's like we are talking to each other in a language the other does not know because we often do not understand each other. I usually start talking to my clients in Turkish for a minute to make the point about how they might have difficulty understanding each other when their lids are not secure.

So, as adults, we need to identify which *Inner Security* tool may help us secure our lids when we are in these different zones. As a general rule, to determine the best self-soothing technique that works for you in different situations, you need to check in with yourself about where your lid is.

For example, when we are in the red zone, somatic tools that calm the primitive parts of our brain are more effective. Techniques that stimulate the vagus nerve, such as 4-7-8 breathing, cold exposure, or physical exercise, can help achieve this rather than cognitive strategies, such as the ABCDE technique.

Most importantly, we need to identify what tools can aid us in staying in the green zone. This way, we can prioritize recharging our batteries. Self-care is not selfish. It enables us to be the most grounded version of ourselves. From this abundant place, we can better support and care for ourselves and others.

This process varies for each person, and to assist you, I recommend completing the chart below with a compilation of items that you believe could aid you in different zones of your nervous system. Please take a moment to revisit the emotion regulation tools we've covered and select the ones you feel align well with your needs for the particular zone.

Feel free to experiment with these techniques at various times to determine when they prove most beneficial for you. Please take your time practicing and consider keeping this chart in a readily accessible location, as it's common to forget effective strategies when overwhelmed.

My *Inner Security* Tools	
Red Zone (Lip Flipped)	
Yellow Zone (Lid Loose)	
Green Zone (Lid Secure)	

Inner Child Needs

Let's consolidate all these reparenting efforts and work on an exercise to help you identify the deeper needs of your Inner Child and find effective ways to fulfill them. This practice involves three columns: the **first** consists of cognitive questions, where you can draw from your knowledge and refer to the Needs Inventory from the Avoidant Part chapter when contemplating the needs of different age brackets. Additionally, I've included a list of possibilities below, compiled with insights from my students and clients, which you may find helpful as a reference. Feel free to add more if you'd like.

Needs we have while growing up:

Food, water, shelter, physical affection (hugs/kisses etc.), encouragement, words of affirmation, emotional validation, identification of feelings, constructive expression of feelings, co-regulation, self-regulation support, socialization, intellectual stimulation, fun, identification of needs, identification of any developmental disorders, cultivating hobbies and interest, encouragement of independent self-care, schedules, honesty, love, acceptance, figuring out interests, future career aspirations identification, mirroring, help to interact with other authority figures, to learn about the unfairness in the world and lack of control in certain situations, understanding consequences, accountability, direct communication skills, sensitivity to differences, cultural humility, awareness about examining biases, intimate conversations (gender identity, sex, drinking, drugs, consent, bystander, etc.), encouragement to include others, peer pressure support, healthy conflict resolution, social media guidance, boundaries, identification of growth areas, patience, understanding when mistakes are made, to learn how to be assertive, permission to ask for support and celebration of successes.

The **second** column has questions that focus more on the heart of your Inner Child. Consider a moment from your childhood from that specific age range for each row and close your eyes. Let your Inner Child appear. There is no rush, so take your time.

Now, open your eyes and use your non-dominant hand, if you are able, to write down the answer in the second column when you ask your Inner Child, "Which of these needs did you need more of growing up?" This will allow your Inner Child to respond more freely than your thinking mind and create space for all of their experiences.

Finally, in the **third** column, answer the question, "How can my *Secure Self* provide these to me?". You don't necessarily need to search for the response; close your eyes or put your gaze down to connect to the higher intelligence within you and allow the answers to come to you.

Ages	What does a child need from caregivers?	Ask your Inner Child: Which of these needs did you need more of growing up?	How can my Secure Self provide these to me?
0-2			
2-5			

Ages	What does a child need from caregivers?	Ask your Inner Child: Which of these needs did you need more of growing up?	How can my Secure Self provide these to me?
5-12			
12-18			

Wonderful job! You now have the big picture of what you need to do to reparent your Inner Child. This process will require patience and consistency, but since it is the most important relationship that we have in life, it is so worth it. There are many helpful books, workbooks, and workshops that you can attend to go deeper into this process and have an intimate connection with your Inner Child. ACA might be a good place to start, where you can practice these skills with fellow travelers on this journey. My clients have benefitted tremendously from this support group.

We will end this chapter with an Inner Child visualization where your *Secure Self* spends a day with them. To begin, imagine a place that brings you joy. This place will be the setting for your reunion with your Inner Child. In the practice below, I have used some of my favorite places in Izmir, my home city. However, feel free to replace them with your favorite places or enjoy this Aegean trip with your Inner Child.

For this visualization, I have chosen my baby self to represent my Inner Child. You can choose any age for your Inner Child. Remember that picture that you took out a while back? That little one might be a good choice for you to reconnect with. Let your imagination run free and explore this new relationship with your Inner Child or Teenager. There are no rules, so have fun and have a lovely day together. The audio recording for this visualization can be accessed on the blog in the *Chapter 14* post (https://medium.com/@securechapters).

Inner Child Visualization

Hello, little baby! Oh, how adorable you are. I really can't take my eyes off you—you have the best smile, and your eyes light up the whole room. I love you so very much. Together, we're going to do something new and exciting. We're going to spend the entire day together having fun in a beautiful summer town called Çeşme. How about that? Are you ready for a relaxing day? Okay, little one, let's take a ride together.

Our first stop is going to be Aya Yorgi Bay. We will have tons of shade by the green trees next to the turquoise water. The Aegean Sea is so beautiful. I will make you a little hammock so you can take a nap. I will be right next to you, rocking you. The breeze is going to make you fall asleep so quickly. To grow, you need a lot of sleep, and I want to make sure you get your rest.

I love you very much, little one. I'm holding you here in my arms. Your skin is so soft and pure. I'm putting on sunscreen even though we are usually under the shade. I am rocking you in my arms, and the birds are helping me to put you to sleep. I'm right here by you, little one. Don't you worry; I will always be here for you, dear one.

As you wake up, we head over to the turquoise-colored water and dip our feet in. You giggle and look at me, wondering if I like it too. I absolutely love it, my little one. The water in this bay is so crystal clear and warm, and I can even see my feet touching the sandy bottom. It's like a massive bathtub! I hold onto you tightly so that you feel safe and secure. Don't worry, I'm right here with you. You love playing in the Aegean Sea, don't you?

Now it's time to eat some delicious food. I'm going to get myself a kumru sandwich, which is so good! We take a leisurely stroll to Ilıca Beach, where we can sit, and I can feed you. You seem hungry, so I make sure you have plenty to eat. As you eat, you gaze out at the beautiful sea.

Once we're done, you see the big sandy beach and want to play. It looks like you got some energy from your food and your nap. It is great that you love playing with the sand and the sea. It is all about what you want and what you don't. We are figuring that out as we go along. We watch the waves here as well. The sound of this peaceful atmosphere and fantastic view relaxes you. It's just so beautiful. You fall asleep in my arms, listening to nature's lullaby.

When you wake up, I will take you to Alaçatı. This place is like a fairy town. I tell you stories about who lived in these two-story old houses and the children who played in these cobblestone streets. The colorful doors of these adorable houses are covered with tiny purple flowers. The people at the little coffee shops and restaurants adore and smile at you. And I noticed you look at things differently, with excitement and wonder. I love that about you.

As the sun goes down and the little candles at the tables are lit, I can see that you're getting tired. I will take you back to our home and put you to sleep. The wind from the Aegean Sea will rock your cradle back and forth, and I will be right by your side, little one. I am looking forward to spending another exciting day with you tomorrow and exploring the world. But for now, sleep well, dear one. I love you.

CHAPTER 15

---✎---

Practicing
Inner Security

It has been more than twenty years since I first met Dr. Tedeschi in Ankara. As you have read, this encounter sparked my interest in positive psychology, which significantly impacted my personal and clinical work (#nerdalert). Now, I would like to introduce another tool from this field that has proven extremely helpful for my clients in enhancing their *Inner Security*.

Many of my clients look at me as if I'm speaking to them in a foreign language when I ask them about their strengths. Since we are more accustomed to focusing on problems and deficiencies, exploring what we are actually good at might seem somewhat unconventional. But we could benefit from cultivating our unique strengths to live well-balanced lives.

Positive psychology researchers have identified 24 character strengths that exist in all of us to varying degrees[1]. These strengths,

Secure

including creativity, kindness, love, and bravery, are considered positive qualities that we all exhibit and can be measured using the VIA Character Strengths Survey[2]. Before we move forward, would you like to take this free online survey with me at https://www.viacharacter.org/account/register?

As a strengths-based practitioner, not only have I been utilizing the VIA survey with my clients, but I have also introduced it to my graduate students, highlighting the benefits of utilizing their strengths. Research shows that exercising character strengths leads to positive mental health[3], improved classroom relationsips[4], motivation in the workplace[5], job performance[6], academic achievement, and well-being[7].

At the beginning of the semester, I encouraged my students to take this survey and spend the semester utilizing their signature strengths (top five character strengths) in their clinical work. We often talked about how they can use these strengths in their supervision.

The results were fantastic. By the end of the semester, my students reported feeling more confident in their clinical skills as future therapists. As authenticity and transparency are important values for me, I also shared my signature strengths with them: appreciation of beauty and excellence, honesty, love of learning, perspective, and humor. This strengths-based approach helped them be more productive in graduate school and lead a more balanced personal and professional life.

In my practice, I often incorporate positive psychology interventions to assist my clients. One of my clients, Ella, struggled with identifying her strengths. When I met her, she worked at a dental office and had lost interest in life. She felt down most days. Ella was a mother of two successful adult children, and her husband passed away four years ago due to a sudden brain aneurysm.

During our sessions, Ella shared that she had been working in the same position for the last fifteen years and had conflicting feelings about applying for a different position within the office. She found it challenging to imagine a different future for herself and feared the possibility of rejection if she applied for the job.

I enjoyed working with Ella because she was caring, considerate, and funny. Our conversations made it evident what a resilient woman she was. Earlier in our work, when I asked her to identify her strengths, the look on her face said, "I have no idea what you are talking about!" She had difficulty spotting what she was good at and noticing all the beautiful qualities she already had. After getting to know her more and delving into some of her goals in therapy, I asked her to take the VIA Character Strengths Survey and bring the results to the next session.

When Ella walked into my office the following week, I noticed she looked slightly different. She was dressed up more than usual and had a big smile. She seemed energized.

As therapists, we value the *here and now* and often use this information to guide our sessions. Therefore, I asked Ella how she had been and complimented her style. Later, I followed up with her and asked her thoughts on the survey.

"I was surprised," she said. "I didn't think about myself in that way."

I was a bit confused and asked, "What do you mean by *that way?*"

"Having so many good things going on for me was a bit weird," she replied. Ella grew up in a household where she wasn't seen much. She was the fifth of the seven children and was very young when she got married.

"Is it hard to take in the positive, Ella?" I asked.

"Yeah, where I come from, it is not very humble to talk about what you are good at," she said.

Ella asked me, "Now, what do we do with these results?"

I appreciate how my clients are willing to grow and change their patterns. "Well," I replied, "out of the 24 strengths, the top five that emerged in your results are your *signature strengths*. These strengths are regularly exhibited in your daily life and make you who you are."

I then asked Ella to tell me her signature strengths, and she was thrilled to discuss the positive aspects of her personality. "Kindness, creativity, gratitude, perseverance, and forgiveness," she read from her results.

During our conversation, we discussed the advantages of exercising her character strengths, particularly her signature ones. Of course, I provided her with research on the benefits of this approach (I know you are very shocked!). I also connected our strengths work to the *Inner Security* work we had been doing. As she began to notice and cultivate her strengths, she became a more **secure base** for herself.

Ella expressed her desire to apply these strengths in her daily life more intentionally. She took her homework assignment on exercising her character strengths seriously. Additionally, I provided her with resources on different ways to use character strengths, which she really enjoyed[8].

In the following weeks, Ella discovered innovative ways to utilize her strengths. Every day, she would ask herself, "How can I use one of my strengths today to make my day better?" Whenever she encountered a challenge, she would ask herself, "Which of my strengths can I use in this situation?" These practices helped her improve her *Inner Security* significantly.

In our sessions, we explored how she could use her strengths to cope with the depressive mood she was experiencing. I shared various research studies with her highlighting the benefits of practicing gratitude[9], one of her signature strengths. Research studies demonstrated the advantages of integrating gratitude into our lives, such as increased psychological well-being[10], self-esteem[10], and happiness[11].

Ella started incorporating gratitude research in her life by keeping a gratitude journal[12], and writing letters to her loved ones expressing gratitude[13]. I shared with her the one-line-a-day journal I found at a small bookstore that can be used for five years. I told her how I used it to write the three things I am grateful for daily. Ella loved the idea and got herself one, too.

We also discussed past experiences where she utilized her strengths and how these instances can help her move forward. All these conversations allowed her to be more encouraging to herself and try new things. This unique way of examining her personality assets opened the door for Ella to have a different perspective on herself. This shift had a ripple effect on her personal and professional life.

As Ella became more aware of her strengths and cultivated them, she became more confident in exploring the world around her. She continued to build her secure base within herself and took calculated risks to further her growth. Ella even went on a date and finally remembered her own badassness.

Through making small but steady changes, she became more in tune with her *Secure Self* and found greater meaning in life. She focused on things that she could control, such as the choices she made daily. This led to significant changes and allowed the depression to lift slowly.

Dr. Sonja Lyubomirsky, in her book, *The How of Happiness: A Scientific Approach to Getting the Life You Want*, explains the research behind how slight and consistent changes can significantly impact our well-being[14]. According to her findings, our genetic makeup determines about 50% of our happiness level. On the other hand, our life circumstances (income, where we live, marital status, age, etc.), which we often believe to be the most important factors, only account for approximately 10% of our overall happiness.

However, the most surprising finding from Dr. Lyubomirsky's research was that 40% of our happiness was related to our day-to-day activities and choices. When Ella saw this happiness pie graph in one of our sessions, she was very intrigued. She realized that our happiness levels are not set in stone, and we can make changes in our lives to help us become happier. It was great to witness positive psychology in action.

Reflection Questions

- What are my signature strengths?

- Which of my strengths bring me joy?

- How can I use my strengths to enhance my happiness?

Now, let's put all that we have learned into practice by completing an exercise in our *Inner Security* journey. Please look at the list of items below and add your possibilities as you wish.

For the next three weeks, I invite you to pick a different item each day and hold yourself accountable for giving yourself this gift. There is an empty chart at the end of the chapter that you can fill out each day as you work on this goal.

This exercise will help you rewire your brain, be your own best ally, and enjoy life. When we utilize the power of neuroplasticity, small incremental changes we make will add up. After completing this challenge, I recommend retaking the *Secure Self Questionnaire* (in the introduction).

My clients, my graduate students, and my graduate students' clients have already started the application and contributed multiple items to this list. Once, we even did this *Inner Security Practice* all together over a semester, which was so much fun. There's power in unity and having shared experiences. So, let's start by showing up for ourselves and feeling the power of walking alongside others on this journey.

Inner Security Practices

Congratulating myself for something on which I improved	Sitting with a cup of tea/coffee and listening to my needs
Enjoying a healthy meal to nourish my body	Leaving the house early to avoid being rushed
Comforting myself when I need soothing	Sending a supportive message to myself (text/email/letter/social media, etc.)
Not using social media for a day	Reading a poem

Writing a poem	Taking a nature walk
Reading a book that I would typically not read	Taking an Epsom salt (or bubble) bath and maybe have some snacks and beverages
Checking in with myself a couple of times per day about how I'm feeling/sensing in my body/thinking	Noticing how my body is doing and what it needs
Exercising (cardio, yoga, t'ai chi, etc.)	Going to a children's movie
Trying something new	Setting a goal for myself
Challenging myself with a small task	Giving myself a foot massage
Meditating for 15 minutes	Setting an intention for my day
Respecting my own decisions and not doubting it	Allowing myself to express my emotions
Going to sleep half an hour early	Taking a dance class that I've been meaning to (e.g., salsa, tango, pole dancing)
Telling a joke	Voicing my opinion even if I am scared
Getting myself a gift	Saying "I love you" to the mirror

I set reminders on my phone to say, "I'm doing the best I can."	Asking myself what I need today to feel that I care about myself
Feeling rain drops on my face	Move my body in a way that makes me feel good. Ex: Riding a bike if I'm able, stretching, etc.
Saying yes to something I would not have before	Expressing gratitude to someone who made an impact on me
Staring at the clouds	Saying, "Thank you, heart, I am safe now."
Taking my dog for a walk and thinking about all the reasons they adore me	Writing in a journal
Drinking water	Noticing three things I am grateful for about myself
Celebrating the completion of a task	Wearing comfy clothes
Floating on water	Visiting somewhere new by myself
Allowing myself to make mistakes and giving myself some slack	Walking on the grass and accepting nature's love
Giving myself a face/neck/ shoulder massage	Doing something silly

Responding to myself with self-compassion when I need	Using one of my strengths in a challenging situation
Watching a sunset/sunrise	Playing with my pet
Drawing my feelings	Coloring/making a mandala
Identifying needs with non-dominant handwriting	Listening to music that soothes my soul
Cooking myself something I love	Trying mindfulness with a regular task (brushing teeth/washing hair, etc.)
Asking for a hug	Wearing something I haven't before
Reading a non-school-related book	Making a mess and letting it sit a while
Lighting candles or using essential oils	Learning more about my family history
Setting aside a time for imagination	Giving myself a pedicure/manicure
Using a face mask	Appreciating different body parts while putting on a lotion
Facetiming someone	Making a list of things that my body does for me
Donating something	Planting flowers

Making your favorite food for yourself	Attending different cultures' festivals/farmers' market
Making time to declutter	Acting on a social justice issue that I care about
Focusing on things that I'm grateful	Waking a bit early to get ready
Talking about things that give me inspiration	Sleeping in
Looking up to the sky regardless of the time of the day	Turning off the clock for a day/weekend
Planning to complete a task I've been avoiding	Making my lunch the night before
Looking at pictures	Picking what I'm going to wear the night before
Social media cleansing	Making my bed in the morning
Going to an Art Museum by myself	Washing bed sheets
Starting one of the projects I've always wanted	Making an appointment that I've been putting off (doctor/dentist/etc.)
Organizing my upcoming week	Getting a massage (acupuncture etc.)

Writing with a crayon for a day	Wearing an outfit that makes me confident
Watching my favorite movie	Listening to my favorite podcast/TED talk
Having sex with myself	Having a good cry
Cleaning my purse/car/wallet	Listening to music I liked during my childhood
Swinging on a swing	Going to the beach and listening to the waves
Sharing a happy memory with someone	Driving in silence
Making peace with someone	Punching a pillow/screaming into a pillow
Standing naked in front of a mirror and appreciating my body	Getting tasks/homework done before the weekend
Leaving a note on the mirror with a mantra	Planning a trip
Playing with a child	Making a vision board
Making plans for my favorite holiday	Making funny faces in the mirror
Taking my favorite supplements/herbs	Making a Zen Garden

Lighting incense	Planning my dream garden
Looking up concerts that I want to attend	Making funny videos with social media tools
Finding a new religious/ spiritual center in my area	Taking selfies with or without funny filters
Looking up new music from my favorite artists	Making a list of my happiest memories
Trying a new recipe	Planning a costume for a holiday or costume party
Buying/making a present for a friend	Looking at pets to adopt from my local shelter or get a gift for my pet
Send myself flowers	Closing my eyes and running my hands all over my body
Watching my favorite childhood cartoon	Playing the soundtrack to my favorite movie/TV show

My Inner Security Practice

My Gift to Myself

Day 1 _ /_/_   _____

Day 2 _ /_/_   _____

Day 3 _ /_/_   _____

Day 4 _ /_/_   _____

Day 5 _ /_/_   _____

Day 6 _ /_/_   _____

Day 7 _ /_/_   _____

Day 8 _ /_/_   _____

Day 9 _ /_/_   _____

Day 10 _ /_/_   _____

Day 11 _ /_/_   _____

Day 12 _ /_/_   _____

Day 13 _ /_/_   _____

Day 14 _ /_/_   _____

Day 15 _ /_/_   _____

Day 16 _ /_/_   _____

Day 17 _ /_/_   _____

Day 18 _ /_/_   _____

Day 19 _ /_/_   _____

Day 20 _ /_/_   _____

Day 21 _ /_/_   _____

CHAPTER 16

Let Your *Secure Self* Be Your Guide

The Sagrada Familia, an architectural wonder in Barcelona, is still under construction after 140 years. Once completed, it is expected to be the tallest basilica in the world. This magnificent building is a testament to continuous growth and transformation.

Just as the Sagrada Familia is evolving, we, too, are works in progress, continually developing and expanding. During my visit to this beautiful building, I was struck by how the colorful glass-stained windows created a mesmerizing dance of light as the sun moved around it. Each part of this structure serves a purpose and comes together to form a stunning work of art, much like our lives and the colorful parts that make us who we are.

Being *Secure* is about understanding and accepting that we are unfinished, imperfect constructions, all exploring this weird thing called life. Our *Secure Self* knows this fact of life and reminds us gently when we forget.

What is Flow?

Newsflash: Being *Secure* doesn't require perfection. We can still lead a fulfilling life with the guidance of our *Secure Self* regardless of where we are in life. This means being in the flow and moving at the same pace as the universe. This is being *Secure*.

When we pause and follow our breath, we are on our way to connecting with our *Secure Self*. When the three parts of our brain are integrated, or in other words, when our lid is secure, we can hear our *Secure Self* and be in the flow. In this unique space, we will receive thoughts, inspiration, and guidance from our *Secure Self*.

Being in the flow means that our *Secure Self* is leading us, and we are not trying to control life. However, this doesn't mean that we are passive. Instead, we understand that we are co-constructors with life. We try our best and accept that life is way bigger than us and has its own movement.

The causes and conditions of life have led to the present moment being as it is. In this space, there is no resistance or grabbing, as Buddhists say. We accept life as it is and do not reject any experience. We are not attached to outcomes but instead focus on the here and now, creating beautiful stepping stones for the future.

Do you remember that scene in *Finding Nemo* where Dory and Marlin swim through the East Australian Current, which was like an underwater highway[1]? That's how it feels to be in the flow. Here, we are not going against the natural lineup of the events that brought us to this point in our lives, but instead, we are swimming with the current of life.

When we are in this flow, things move with ease. There are no questions like "Where am I going?" or "How will I get there?" It's all about enjoying the effortless nature of this ride and suddenly realizing that you are much closer to where you need to be.

When we reconnect with our *Secure Self*, life becomes an adventure. We can relax into this wonderful current. We can learn to allow our *Secure Self* to lead us and not freak out when we're out of the flow.

Life is a master class for practicing being in and out of this flow. When we are out of the flow, we can take a step back and choose not to take any immediate action. (Oh my goodness, isn't this the most challenging part since we usually want to fix and solve things right away?) Instead, we can focus on doing things that make us feel better by attending to our nervous system needs and waiting until we feel in the flow again.

Sometimes, our Anxious or Avoidant Parts try to control the outcomes in life, going against the flow and trying to prove our worthiness or help us feel safer. Unfortunately, this often leaves us feeling isolated, stuck, and hopeless, burdened by uncertainty and unpredictability.

It's easy to slip into the belief that this state will last forever and we'll be miserable for the rest of our lives. But it's important to remember that we have a *Secure Self* that can care for those parts and that we are safe. It's okay to get out of the flow sometimes; it's just part of being human.

In this space, we can remind ourselves:

"I'm going to be able to handle whatever comes my way, but right now, I'm too driven by my Anxious/Avoidant Part. These parts are just trying to control life, and life has its intelligence that we cannot control.

These parts want to protect me from further harm. They have good intentions, but their delivery is terrible, making me feel disconnected from my *Secure Self*.

So, I need to hold off, take a step back, and wait. I will now focus on what makes me feel better. I will practice some of my *Inner*

Security tools to get back into the flow. Figuring things out will be much smoother when I'm back in the flow."

This step is an essential piece of the puzzle. When we notice that we are not in the flow, we can be the observer of this experience. We can then allow our *Secure Self* to guide us and tend to our different parts. Let's do an exercise where we practice this process. The audio recording for this visualization is on the blog in the *Chapter 16* post (https://medium.com/@securechapters).

Secure Self Visualization

Please find a comfortable position, either sitting or lying down. Close your eyes or turn your gaze downwards and start the process of turning inward. Slowly begin focusing on your breath. Breathe in and breathe out. Breathe in and breathe out. Inhale and exhale. Notice what your body is in contact with at the moment. Bring your attention to here and now. Allow your body, mind, emotions, and spirit to connect.

Now, think of a challenging situation that you have recently struggled with. Choose a problem up to a 2 or 3 on a scale of 1 to 10, nothing too significant. Focus on it and see where your mind takes you. Your Anxious or Avoidant Part will let you know what it needs help with. Just take a minute to receive the situation.

Now, I would like you to imagine two chairs facing each other. Pick whatever style, color, and size of chairs you'd like in your imagination. There is no right or wrong in this. Next, I'd like you to imagine your Secure Self sitting in one of these chairs. Just let your imagination do the work.

For the other chair, I'd like you to invite either your Anxious or Avoidant Parts, struggling with the challenging situation, and ask that part to take a seat. We will be asking that specific part to have a dialogue with the Secure Self. You can include both parts in the conversation in the future, but for now, let's start with just one.

Begin by letting the part with a stronger voice take the lead. Let either the Anxious or the Avoidant Part tell what it needs to tell. There is no time limit, so let it explain what is happening and give its perspective.

Listen carefully when it expresses doubts or fears or asks questions. Take some time to let this part of you express everything it is thinking, feeling, struggling with, and wondering about without judgment. Be open and receptive to its words, honoring them. Let it know that it is being heard and seen. Take a few minutes to make sure all is expressed.

Now, it's time to let your Secure Self respond. Bring forth all the qualities of your Secure Self—loving, embracing, engaging, available, responsive, optimistic, soothing, compassionate, reassuring, supportive, sensitive, kind, caring, and accepting.

Connect with your Secure Self and let it talk to this other part of you. Allow its incredible compassion to come through in its words. Listen to it as it comforts and provides a safe haven for the Anxious or Avoidant Part of you. What is it saying? How is it mirroring, validating, and reflecting the discomfort of the Anxious or Avoidant Part?

You might hear your Secure Self say, "I know this is really hard. You are not alone. I am here for you. I'm glad you are here. You are so valuable and so worthy. You are special to me. I see you, and I hear you. Thank you for letting me know of all of this. I am here now."

Let this conversation continue naturally in your mind for a few minutes. Just observe this lovely interaction.

Now, notice how your Anxious or Avoidant Part responds to these words. Does it have anything more to say? If so, allow it to speak up and be available to listen. This Part is not used to hearing these words, so it might take some time to receive from your Secure Self and process. That's perfectly okay. Remember, it will take more than one time to practice this new way.

If more hearing or seeing needs to be done by the Secure Self, let that process take place. Notice what that Anxious or Avoidant Part really needs. Attend to those needs. What is the core negative belief that this part has about itself? What is it saying when struggling? What does it tell you? I am...what? See what that belief underneath the struggle it's dealing with is.

For example, does it feel unworthy, unlovable, or inadequate? Notice the anxious or avoidant thoughts or feelings that are coming up. They are there for a reason; now you see and hear them.

Now, allow your Secure Self to address that belief with kindness and love. Those thoughts or feelings are welcomed and accepted. Notice how your body responds to this newfound attentiveness and responsiveness.

Now, bring the conversation from the mind to the heart. Let them have a heart-to-heart talk. See the pain, and let the Secure Self comfort the pain. Trust the process. Your Secure Self knows what to say and how to help. Your Secure Self knows the way. Make sure nothing is unsaid at this point.

Take a deep breath and notice how this Inner Security feels.

More and more, I am learning to attend to my Anxious and Avoidant Parts and be there for them. More and more, I'm learning what my body, mind, emotions, and spirit need and starting to provide those to myself. More and more, I am receiving from the loving, embracing, and engaging Secure Self.

And when you are ready, come back to here and now.

Secure Self Exploration

I hope you enjoyed allowing your *Secure Self* to care for your Anxious and Avoidant Parts. Now that we have reconnected with our *Secure*

Self, let's take some time to reflect on its other aspects waiting to be discovered. Please complete the sentences below to continue exploring your *Secure Self*.

My Secure Self's qualities are: _____

_____

My Secure Self's values are: _____

_____

My Secure Self's intentions are: _____

_____

My Secure Self's definition of self-love is: _____

_____

My Secure Self's definition of self-compassion is: _____

_____

My Secure Self's self-acceptance feels like: _____

_____

My Secure Self's needs are: _____

_____

My Secure Self's strengths are: _____

_____

My Secure Self calms me down by: _____

_____

My Secure Self's definition of being Secure is: _____

_____

Wonderful, dear one; I'm so proud of us for doing this deep inner work. Our transformation will be an ongoing process as our consciousness expands. I hope we can learn to trust the current and allow ourselves to flow with it. From this place, we can help extend the universe while enjoying being human. This is what being *Secure* means.

Thank you for coming on this journey with me. I so appreciate your presence and support in my heart. Thank you for being who you are and being open to listening to this imperfect human being.

As we near the end of this book, I am feeling emotional. However, I believe that we will connect again in the future. Before we part ways, let's do one last visualization and allow our *Secure Self* to guide us. You can listen to the audio recording of this visualization on the blog in the *Chapter 16* post (https://medium.com/@securechapters), and I would recommend bilateral tapping with it.

Secure Self Guidance Visualization

Let's start by closing your eyes or dropping your gaze down. Take a deep breath, slow your breathing, and feel your mind settle. There is nothing urgent or pressing right now. You have nothing to attend to and no tasks to complete—you can just enjoy some time with yourself. Inhale and exhale deeply, and let go of any residual stress from your day. This time is just for you.

Now, focus on your intention to connect to your Secure Self. You have already met and gained wisdom and guidance from your Secure Self. And now it is waiting for you to discover it even more. Just remember how you were born with your Secure Self.

If you have made some connection with your Secure Self, that is wonderful. However, if you are struggling with it, that is okay, too. You can take your time and focus on the intention of being guided by your Secure Self when you are ready. There is no need to rush. We all blossom in our own unique timeline. If you need help with this connection right now, this is a great time to practice being kind to yourself and accept exactly where you are waiting to blossom.

Let's notice our breath again or any other anchor you have chosen. This anchor can help us turn our attention inward and connect with our loving, Secure Self.

Our Secure Self is connected to the universe; it comes from the universe and goes to the universe.

Our Secure Self gives us the answers that we are looking for. Our Secure Self is part of the universe; by accessing it, we can find the answers we seek. We all have this inner knowing, and we can tap into it by quieting our minds and opening our hearts.

Now, let's imagine a life where the Secure Self gently leads you into your desired life. How would your life look if your Secure Self was in the driver's seat? What would you be doing? What would you be focusing on? How would you love? How would you be? Most importantly, how would you be treating yourself? Let's ponder these questions in this beautiful silence.

Just soak in this way of living life. This is where you treat yourself like a gem; you are opening yourself up to new experiences and being patient with yourself. You show yourself compassion when you need support and acknowledge your strengths. You listen to your intuition, you are there for yourself, and you encourage yourself to stretch even more. Just allow yourself to be with this possibility for a little while.

Your Secure Self has values, intentions, and qualities that will help you live your life from an open-hearted place. Take a few more minutes to enjoy this moment and be in the flow.

Now, slowly bring your attention back to your breath as you open your eyes and smile as you welcome yourself back to the present.

Conclusion

Looking back, I can see how my *Secure Self* guided me to the Whale's Tail in Uvita, Costa Rica. I just had to learn to listen. While sitting down on the rocks in this marvelous beach extension in the middle of the ocean and listening to the powerful waves, I suddenly realized how life has its own ways of working.

I had tried to see the Whale's Tail before, but the high tide had prevented me from doing so. It took me several trips to realize that the ocean's tides didn't operate according to *my* schedule. Life seemed far wiser than my limited ways of understanding and conditioning.

As I gazed at both sides of the beach from the end of the tail, I was overcome by a striking sensation of my past and future converging into the present. As the ocean gradually rose, I sensed my Avoidant and Anxious Parts slowly dissolving and merging until they became one. My *Secure Self*, the vast ocean of consciousness, was taking over, and the fragmented parts of my being were becoming whole.

I was *Secure*.

Dear one, it is now time to say goodbye. I'm so grateful to have spent this time with you, where we were able to reconnect with our *Secure Self,* understand our different parts, and develop various ways to lead a more authentic and vibrant life. Together, we have taken responsibility for ourselves and found the courage to tend to our deep wounds and practice self-compassion. We are committed to constructing a brighter future with the help of our new *Inner Security* tools. We can now allow our *Secure Self* to guide our lives, travel to new places we have never imagined, and feel *Inner Security.*

May we all accept that what had occurred in the past when we were children was not our fault. May we hold those memories with tenderness, kindness, and love in our hearts. May we all extend the gift of compassion to those parts of ourselves that we once considered flawed or unworthy. May we reconnect to our *Secure Self* and let it care for these vulnerable parts. May we remember that we are from the same source. May we all find the courage to keep expanding our consciousness.

Let's remember that our *Secure Self* gives us permission to make mistakes. We don't have to be perfect anymore. We can have healthy boundaries and grow with self-compassion. We can release the illusion of control, and we can ask for help from life. Together, we are learning to trust, accept, and allow. We are discovering how to be in the flow.

Before you go, please take this acronym to help you connect with your *Secure Self.* **LEE.**

Loving is the antidote to fear,

Embracing is the antidote to anxiety, and

Engaging is the antidote to avoidance.

LEE.

This is our work.

As you continue your journey, you will find that it becomes deeper and more fulfilling. By *Loving* your Inner Child and reparenting securely, you will gain strength and confidence. *Embracing* your truth, strengths, and yourself will be the remedy to soothe the Anxious Part. *Engaging* with your emotions and trying new things will energize and motivate the Avoidant Part.

You will break the vicious intergenerational cycles one day at a time and *Securely* relate to yourself and others. On this exciting, scary, less-traveled journey, notice the presence of your *Secure Self* and remember that the more *Inner Security* tools you practice, the more you will feel inner peace.

When we let go and accept what is, we make friends with uncertainty and begin to feel those serendipitous touches on our souls. Life is precious and fragile. With the sudden and unexpected deaths of Lee, Lily, my dear therapist, and two high school friends, I learned that any moment could be our last. So why not savor the *now*?

Thank you again for being with me. I am rejuvenated by writing and practicing what I have shared with you in this book. And as a fellow traveler on this incredible journey, it was my honor to travel with you and be with you in your transformation.

Okay, okay, I'm finally putting the tissue down. I'm just really savoring the gratitude I feel toward life and you. Just before we go, let's do our final **LEE** meditation and experience the presence of our *Secure Self*. The *Conclusion* post on the blog contains the audio recording for this meditation (https://medium.com/@securechapters).

Until next time, take good care of yourself, dear one!

Lee Meditation

Please get into a comfortable position and close your eyes or turn your gaze down. Let's take several deep breaths and reflect on the journey that you have been on. Along the way, you remembered many things you had forgotten about yourself, but, most importantly, you remembered your Secure Self.

On your travels, you started constructing your new future by practicing optimism, identifying your strengths, soothing your Inner Child, and allowing self-compassion to be your inner resource. You learned to be your own secure base and safe haven. And you did all this while breaking the vicious intergenerational cycles and welcoming all your emotions.

Now, you are closer to yourself than ever. You are resilient as you recognize how much you have already survived. You are more loving toward yourself as you see your wounds. You are freer than you were before because you have Inner Security.

You have embarked on a fantastic journey where you reconnect with your Secure Self. Remember, dear one; you were Secure when you were born. Life might have gotten in the way, and you may have forgotten that. And that's alright because you remember now.

Please continue letting your Secure Self be your guide, dear one. Please remember that you are never alone, that you have a message people need to hear, and that you are valuable.

Take a moment to thank your Anxious and Avoidant Parts for keeping you safe so far. Let them know that you now have your Secure Self to rely on. And then watch how your Secure Self takes care of the Anxious and Avoidant Parts. How compassionate, attentive, and sensitive the Secure Self is when approaching the other parts. Remember to practice LEE: loving, embracing, and engaging.

Remember this feeling, dear one. When things feel like they are falling apart again, return to this moment. Remember this feeling of unconditionally loving, embracing, and engaging who you are. This is your core inner resource that no one can take away from you. Remember who you are and celebrate who you are.

Now, notice the Inner Security you feel. You are so courageous to take this journey to connect with your Secure Self again. Notice how you are starting to relax into life. There is no more fighting anymore. You've gotten out of the hole and realized you are already whole. You are safe. You are worthy. You are Secure.

References

Introduction

1. Associated Press. (2019, August 7). *Tony Morrison's most notable quotes about life, race and storytelling.* USA Today. https://www.usatoday.com/story/entertainment/books/2019/08/07/toni-morrison-nobel-prize-winning-writer-most-notable-quotes/1941628001/

Chapter 1

1. Siegel, E. (2022, February 3). *How many stars are in the universe?* Big Think. https://bigthink.com/starts-with-a-bang/how-many-stars/
2. Burbidge, E. M., Burbidge, G. R., Fowler, W. A., & Hoyle, F. (1957). Synthesis of the elements in stars. *Reviews of Modern Physics, 29*(4), 547–650. https://doi.org/10.1103/revmodphys.29.547
3. Howard, R. (Director). (1995). *Apollo 13* [Film]. Universal Pictures, Imagine Entertainment.
4. National Human Genome Research Institute. (n.d). *Human genomic variation.* https://www.genome.gov/about-genomics/educational-resources/fact-sheets/human-genomic-variation

Chapter 2

1. Rumi, J. M. (2005). *Rumi: The book of love: Poems of ecstasy and longing* (C. Barks, Trans). Harper One.
2. Pernet, C. R., Belov, N., Delorme, A., & Zammit, A. (2021). Mindfulness related changes in grey matter: A systematic review and

meta–analysis. *Brain Imaging and Behavior, 15*, 2720–2730. https://
doi.org/10.1007/s11682-021-00453-4

3. Edwards, M. K., & Loprinzi, P. D. (2018). Comparative effects of
    meditation and exercise on physical and psychosocial health outcomes:
    A review of randomized controlled trials. *Postgraduate Medicine,
    130*(2), 222–228. https://doi.org/10.1080/00325481.2018.1409049

4. Potes, A., Souza, G., Nikolitch, K., Penheiro, R., Moussa, Y.,
    Jarvis, E., Looper, K., & Rej, S. (2018). Mindfulness in severe and
    persistent mental illness: A systematic review. *International Journal of
    Psychiatry in Clinical Practice, 22*(4), 253–261. https://doi.org/10.10
    80/13651501.2018.1433857

5. Kwekkeboom, K. L., & Bratzke, L. C. (2016). A systematic review
    of relaxation, meditation, and guided imagery strategies for symptom
    management in heart failure. *The Journal of Cardiovascular Nursing,
    31*(5), 457–468. https://doi.org/10.1097/JCN.0000000000000274

6. Dunn, C., Haubenreiser, M., Johnson, M., Nordby, K., Aggarwal,
    S., Myer, S., & Thomas, C. (2018). Mindfulness approaches and
    weight loss, weight maintenance, and weight regain. *Current Obesity
    Reports, 7*(1), 37–49. https://doi.org/10.1007/s13679-018-0299-6

7. Davidson, R. J., Kabat-Zinn, J., Schumacher, J., Rosenkranz, M.,
    Muller, D., Santorelli, S. F., Urbanowski, F., Harrington, A., Bonus,
    K., & Sheridan, J. F. (2003). Alterations in brain and immune
    function produced by mindfulness meditation. *Psychosomatic
    Medicine, 65*(4), 564–570. https://doi.org/10.1097/01.
    psy.0000077505.67574.e3

8. Norris, C. J., Creem, D., Hendler, R., & Kober, H. (2018). Brief
    mindfulness meditation improves attention in novices: Evidence
    from ERPs and moderation by neuroticism. *Frontiers in Human
    Neuroscience, 12*, 1–20. https://doi.org/10.3389/fnhum.2018.00315

9. Shiba, K., Nishimoto, M., Sugimoto, M., & Ishikawa, Y. (2015). The association between meditation practice and job performance: A cross-sectional study. *PloS One, 10*(5), e0128287. https://doi.org/10.1371/journal.pone.0128287

10. Chaix, R., Alvarez-López, M. J., Fagny, M., Lemee, L., Regnault, B., Davidson, R. J., Lutz, A., & Kaliman, P. (2017). Epigenetic clock analysis in long-term meditators. *Psychoneuroendocrinology, 85,* 210–214. https://doi.org/10.1016/j.psyneuen.2017.08.016

Chapter 3

1. Nottebohm, F. (1981). A brain for all seasons: Cyclical anatomical changes in song control nuclei of the canary brain. *Science, 214*(4527), 1368–1370. https://doi.org/10.1126/science.7313697

2. Maguire, E. A., Gadian, D. G., Johnsrude, I. S., Good, C. D., Ashburner, J., J. Frackowiak, R. S., & Frith, C. D. (2000). Navigation-related structural change in the hippocampi of taxi drivers. *Proceedings of the National Academy of Sciences of the United States of America, 97*(8), 4398–4403. https://doi.org/10.1073/pnas.070039597

3. Konorski, J. (1948). *Conditioned reflexes and neuron organization.* Cambridge University Press.

4. Hebb, D.O. (1949). *The Organization of behavior.* Wiley & Sons.

5. Center for Healthy Minds (n.d). *Our history.* https://centerhealthyminds.org/about/overview

6. Brefczynski-Lewis, J. A., Lutz, A., Schaefer, H. S., Levinson, D. B., & Davidson, R. J. (2007). Neural correlates of attentional expertise in long-term meditation practitioners. *Proceedings of the National Academy of Sciences of the United States of America, 104*(27), 11483–11488. https://doi.org/10.1073/pnas.0606552104

7. Davidson, R. J., & Lutz, A. (2008). Buddha's brain: Neuroplasticity and meditation. *IEEE Signal Processing Magazine, 25*(1), 176–174. https://doi.org/10.1109/msp.2008.4431873

8. Rozin, P., & Royzman, E. B. (2001). Negativity bias, negativity dominance, and contagion. *Personality and Social Psychology Review, 5*(4), 296–320. https://doi.org/10.1207/S15327957PSPR0504_2

9. Waxenbaum JA, Reddy V, Varacallo M. Anatomy, Autonomic Nervous System. [Updated 2023 Jul 24]. In: StatPearls [Internet]. Treasure Island (FL): StatPearls Publishing; 2024 Jan-. Available from: https://www.ncbi.nlm.nih.gov/books/NBK539845/

10. Lake, J. I., & Heuckeroth, R. O. (2013). Enteric nervous system development: Migration, differentiation, and disease. *American Journal of Physiology. Gastrointestinal and liver physiology, 305*(1), G1–G24. https://doi.org/10.1152/ajpgi.00452.2012

11. Van der Kolk, B. (2015). *The body keeps the score: Brain, mind, and body in the healing of trauma.* Penguin Books.

12. Frankl, V. E. (1959). *Man's search for meaning.* Beacon Press.

13. TED. (2011, January 3). *The power of vulnerability* [Video]. Youtube. https://www.youtube.com/watch?v=iCvmsMzlF7o

Chapter 4

1. Nelson, P. (2012). *There's a hole in my sidewalk: The romance of self-love discovery.* Beyond Words/Atria Books.

2. Tedeschi, R. G., & Calhoun, L. G. (1996). The posttraumatic growth inventory: Measuring the positive legacy of trauma. *Journal of Traumatic Stress, 9*(3), 455– 471. https://doi.org/10.1007/BF02103658

3. Arkar, H., Sorias, O., Tunca, Z., Aklin, T., Akdede, B., Sahin, S., Akvardar, Y., Sari, O., Ozerdem, A., & Cimilli, C. (2005).

Factorial structure, validity and reliability of the Turkish temperament and character inventory. *Turkish Journal of Psychiatry, 16*(3), 190-204.

Chapter 5

1. Cellier, D., Riddle, J., Petersen, I., & Hwang, K. (2021). The development of theta and alpha neural oscillations from ages 3 to 24 years. *Developmental Cognitive Neuroscience, 50,* 100969. https://doi.org/10.1016/j.dcn.2021.100969
2. Ainsworth, M. S., & Bowlby, J. (1991). An ethological approach to personality development. *American Psychologist, 46*(4), 333–341. https://doi.org/10.1037/0003-066X.46.4.333
3. Bowlby, J. (1983). *Attachment and loss. Vol. 1: Attachment.* Basic Books.
4. Ainsworth, M. D. S., & Bell, S. M. (1970). Attachment, exploration, and separation: Illustrated by the behavior of one-year-olds in a strange situation. *Child Development, 41*(1), 49–67. https://doi.org/10.2307/1127388
5. Main, M., & Solomon, J. (1986). Discovery of a new, insecure-disorganized/disoriented attachment pattern. In M. W. Yogman & T. B. Brazelton (Eds.), *Affective development in infancy* (pp. 95–124). Ablex Publishing.
6. Hazan, C., & Shaver, P. (1987). Romantic love conceptualized as an attachment process. *Journal of Personality and Social Psychology, 52*(3), 511– 524. https://doi.org/10.1037/0022-3514.52.3.511
7. Bartholomew, K., & Horowitz, L. M. (1991). Attachment styles among young adults: A test of a four-category model. *Journal of Personality and Social Psychology, 61*(2), 226–244. https://doi.org/10.1037//0022-3514.61.2.226

Chapter 6

1. Centers for Disease Control and Prevention. (n.d). *About the CDC-Kaiser ACE study.* https://www.cdc.gov/violenceprevention/aces/about.html

2. Swedo, E. A., Aslam, M. V., Dahlberg, L. L., Niolon, P. H., Guinn, A. S., Simon, T. R., & Mercy, J. A. (2023). Prevalence of adverse childhood experiences among U.S. adults — Behavioral risk factor surveillance system, 2011–2020. *Morbidity and Mortality Weekly Report, 72*(26), 707–715. http://dx.doi.org/10.15585/mmwr.mm7226a2

3. Van der Kolk, B. (2015). *The body keeps the score: Brain, mind, and body in the healing of trauma.* Penguin Books.

4. Rothschild, B. (2000). *The body remembers: The psychophysiology of trauma and trauma treatment.* W. W. Norton & Company.

5. Felitti V. J. (2002). The relation between adverse childhood experiences and adult health: Turning gold into lead. *The Permanente Journal, 6*(1), 44–47.

6. Dube, S. R., Anda, R. F., Felitti, V. J., Edwards, V. J., & Croft, J. B. (2002). Adverse childhood experiences and personal alcohol abuse as an adult. *Addictive Behaviors, 27*(5), 713–725. https://doi.org/10.1016/s0306-4603(01)00204-0

7. Ford, E. S., Anda, R. F., Edwards, V. J., Perry, G. S., Zhao, G., Li, C., & Croft, J. B. (2011). Adverse childhood experiences and smoking status in five states. *Preventive medicine, 53*(3), 188–193. https://doi.org/10.1016/j.ypmed.2011.06.015

8. Forster, M., Gower, A. L., Borowsky, I. W., & McMorris, B. J. (2017). Associations between adverse childhood experiences, student-teacher relationships, and non- medical use of prescription medications among adolescents. *Addictive behaviors, 68*, 30–34. https://doi.org/10.1016/j.addbeh.2017.01.004

9. Brown, D. W., Anda, R. F., Tiemeier, H., Felitti, V. J., Edwards, V. J., Croft, J. B., & Giles, W. H. (2009). Adverse childhood experiences and the risk of premature mortality. *American Journal of Preventive Medicine, 37*(5), 389–396. https://doi.org/10.1016/j.amepre.2009.06.021

10. Yehuda, R., Daskalakis, N. P., Bierer, L. M., Bader, H. N., Klengel, T., Holsboer, F., & Binder, E. B. (2016). Holocaust exposure induced intergenerational effects on FKBP5 methylation. *Biological Psychiatry, 80*(5), 372–380. https://doi.org/10.1016/j.biopsych.2015.08.005

Chapter 7

1. Waxenbaum JA, Reddy V, Varacallo M. Anatomy, Autonomic Nervous System. [Updated 2023 Jul 24]. In: StatPearls [Internet]. Treasure Island (FL): StatPearls Publishing; 2024 Jan-. Available from: https://www.ncbi.nlm.nih.gov/books/NBK539845/

2. Siegel, D. (2015, July 24). *Daniel Siegel hand model* [Video]. Youtube. https://www.youtube.com/watch?v=qFTljLo1bK8

3. Howland R. H. (2014). Vagus nerve stimulation. *Current Behavioral Neuroscience Reports, 1*(2), 64–73. https://doi.org/10.1007/s40473-014-0010-5

4. Mason, H., Vandoni, M., Debarbieri, G., Codrons, E., Ugargol, V., & Bernardi, L. (2013). Cardiovascular and respiratory effect of yogic slow breathing in the yoga beginner: What is the best approach? *Evidence-Based Complementary and Alternative Medicine, 2013,* 743504. https://doi.org/10.1155/2013/743504

5. Mäkinen, T. M., Mäntysaari, M., Pääkkönen, T., Jokelainen, J., Palinkas, L. A., Hassi, J., Leppäluoto, J., Tahvanainen, K., & Rintamäki, H. (2008). Autonomic nervous function during whole-

body cold exposure before and after cold acclimation. *Aviation, Space, and Environmental Medicine, 79*(9), 875–882. https://doi.org/10.3357/asem.2235.2008

6. Vickhoff, B., Malmgren, H., Aström, R., Nyberg, G., Ekström, S. R., Engwall, M., Snygg, J., Nilsson, M., & Jörnsten, R. (2013). Music structure determines heart rate variability of singers. *Frontiers in Psychology, 4,* 334. https://doi.org/10.3389/fpsyg.2013.00334

7. Khattab, K., Khattab, A. A., Ortak, J., Richardt, G., & Bonnemeier, H. (2007). Iyengar yoga increases cardiac parasympathetic nervous modulation among healthy yoga practitioners. *Evidence-Based Complementary and Alternative Medicine, 4*(4), 511–517. https://doi.org/10.1093/ecam/nem087

8. Chang, R. Y., Koo, M., Yu, Z. R., Kan, C. B., Chu, I. T., Hsu, C. T., & Chen, C. Y. (2008). The effect of t'ai chi exercise on autonomic nervous function of patients with coronary artery disease. *Journal of Alternative and Complementary Medicine, 14*(9), 1107–1113. https://doi.org/10.1089/acm.2008.0166

9. Meier, M., Unternaehrer, E., Dimitroff, S. J., Benz, A. B. E., Bentele, U. U., Schorpp, S. M., Wenzel, M., & Pruessner, J. C. (2020). Standardized massage interventions as protocols for the induction of psychophysiological relaxation in the laboratory: A block randomized, controlled trial. *Scientific Reports, 10*(1), 14774. https://doi.org/10.1038/s41598-020-71173-w

10. Telles, S., Raghavendra, B. R., Naveen, K. V., Manjunath, N. K., Kumar, S., & Subramanya, P. (2013). Changes in autonomic variables following two meditative states described in yoga texts. *Journal of Alternative and Complementary Medicine, 19*(1), 35–42. https://doi.org/10.1089/acm.2011.0282

11. Kai, S., Nagino, K., Ito, T., Oi, R., Nishimura, K., Morita, S., & Yaoi, R. (2016). Effectiveness of moderate intensity

interval training as an index of autonomic nervous activity. *Rehabilitation Research and Practice, 2016,* 6209671. https://doi. org/10.1155/2016/6209671

12. Dolgoff-Kaspar, R., Baldwin, A., Johnson, M. S., Edling, N., & Sethi, G. K. (2012). Effect of laughter yoga on mood and heart rate variability in patients awaiting organ transplantation: A pilot study. *Alternative therapies in health and medicine, 18*(5), 61–66.

13. He, W., Wang, X., Shi, H., Shang, H., Li, L., Jing, X., & Zhu, B. (2012). Auricular acupuncture and vagal regulation. *Evidence-Based Complementary and Alternative Medicine, 2012,* 786839. https://doi. org/10.1155/2012/786839

14. Kok, B. E., Coffey, K. A., Cohn, M. A., Catalino, L. I., Vacharkulksemsuk, T., Algoe, S. B., Brantley, M., & Fredrickson, B. L. (2013). How positive emotions build physical health: Perceived positive social connections account for the upward spiral between positive emotions and vagal tone. *Psychological Science, 24*(7), 1123–1132. https://doi.org/10.1177/0956797612470827

15. Yoga With Adriene. (n.d.). *Yoga with Adriene Videos* [Video]. Youtube. https://www.youtube.com/@yogawithadriene/videos

16. HeartMath Institute. (n.d). *Our vision.* https://www.heartmath.org/

17. Laborde, S., Mosley, E., & Thayer, J. F. (2017). Heart rate variability and cardiac vagal tone in psychophysiological research - recommendations for experiment planning, data analysis, and data reporting. *Frontiers in Psychology, 8,* 213. https://doi.org/10.3389/ fpsyg.2017.00213

18. HeartMath Institute. (n.d). *Inner balance and emWave.* https://store. heartmath.org/Inner- Balance-Sensor/

19. Muse. (n.d). *Train your brain and find your focus.* https:// choosemuse.com/

20. Adult Children of Alcoholics and Dysfunctional Families World Service Organization. (n.d). *Welcome to adult children of alcoholics & dysfunctional families.* https://adultchildren.org/

21. Adult Children of Alcoholics and Dysfunctional Families World Service Organization. (n.d). *Laundry list.* https://adultchildren.org/literature/laundry-list/

Chapter 8

1. Willcox, G. (1982). The feeling wheel: A tool for expanding awareness of emotions and increasing spontaneity and intimacy. *Transactional Analysis Journal, 12*(4), 274–276. https://doi.org/10.1177/036215378201200411

2. Torrisi, S. J., Lieberman, M. D., Bookheimer, S. Y., & Altshuler, L. L. (2013). Advancing understanding of affect labeling with dynamic causal modeling. *NeuroImage, 82*, 481–488. https://doi.org/10.1016/j.neuroimage.2013.06.025

3. The Center for Nonviolent Communication. (n.d). *Feelings and needs inventory.* https://www.cnvc.org/store/feelings-and-needs-inventory

Chapter 9

1. Guvenatam, O. (Executive Producer). (2022-present). *Another self.* [TV series]. OGM Pictures.

Chapter 10

1. Seligman, M. E. P. (2006). *Learned optimism: How to change your mind and your life.* Vintage.

2. Seligman, M. E. P., & Csikszentmihalyi, M. (2000). Positive psychology: An introduction. *American Psychologist, 55*(1), 5–14. https://doi.org/10.1037/0003- 066X.55.1.5

3. Abramson, L. Y., Seligman, M. E., & Teasdale, J. D. (1978). Learned helplessness in humans: Critique and reformulation. *Journal of Abnormal Psychology, 87*(1), 49–74. https://doi.org/10.1037/0021-843X.87.1.49

4. Ellis, A. (1957). Rational psychotherapy and individual psychology. *Journal of Individual Psychology, 13*, 38–44.

5. Ellis, A. (1991). The revised ABC's of rational-emotive therapy (RET). *Journal of Rational-Emotive & Cognitive-Behavior Therapy, 9*(3), 139–172. https://doi.org/10.1007/BF01061227

6. Beck, A. T. (1970). Cognitive therapy: Nature and relation to behavior therapy. *Behavior Therapy, 1*(2), 184–200. https://doi.org/10.1016/S0005-7894(70)80030-2

7. Beck, A. T. (1963). Thinking and depression: I. Idiosyncratic content and cognitive distortions. *Archives of General Psychiatry, 9*(4), 324–333. https://doi.org/10.1001/archpsyc.1963.01720160014002

8. Beck, A. T., Rush, A. J., Shaw, B. F., & Emery, G. (1987). *Cognitive therapy of depression*. The Guilford Press.

9. Sahin, Z. S., Nalbone, D. P., Wetchler, J. L., & Bercik, J. M. (2010). The relationship of differentiation, family coping skills, and family functioning with optimism in college-age students. *Contemporary Family Therapy: An International Journal, 32*(3), 238–256. https://doi.org/10.1007/s10591-010-9116-4

10. UC Berkley. (2016, May 16). *Sheryl Sandberg gives UC Berkeley commencement keynote speech*. [Video]. Youtube. https://www.youtube.com/watch?v=iqm-XEqpayc

11. Sandberg, S., & Grant, A. (2017). *Option B: Facing adversity, building resilience, and finding joy*. Knopf.

Chapter 11

1. Sprenkle, D. H., & Blow, A. J. (2004). Common factors and our sacred models. *Journal of Marital and Family Therapy, 30*(2), 113–129. https://doi.org/10.1111/j.1752-0606.2004.tb01228.x

2. Neff, K. D. (2003). Development and validation of a scale to measure self-compassion. *Self and Identity, 2,* 223–250. https://doi.org/10.1080/15298860309027

3. Neff, K. D. (2003). Self-compassion: An alternative conceptualization of a healthy attitude toward oneself. *Self and Identity, 2,* 85–102. https://doi.org/10.1080/15298860309032

4. Neff, K. D. (2011). *Self-Compassion: The proven power of being kind to yourself.* William Morrow.

5. Neff, K. D. & Germer, C. K (2018). *The Mindful self-compassion workbook: A proven way to accept yourself, find inner strength, and thrive.* The Guilford Press.

6. Luo, X., Che, X., Lei, Y., & Li, H. (2021). Investigating the influence of self- compassion-focused interventions on posttraumatic stress: A systematic review and meta-analysis. *Mindfulness, 12(12),* 2865–2876. https://doi.org/10.1007/s12671-021-01732-3

7. Hiraoka, R., Meyer, E. C., Kimbrel, N. A., DeBeer, B. B., Gulliver, S. B., & Morissette, S. B. (2015). Self-Compassion as a prospective predictor of PTSD symptom severity among trauma-exposed U.S. Iraq and Afghanistan war veterans. *Journal of traumatic stress, 28*(2), 127–133. https://doi.org/10.1002/jts.21995

8. Millet, N., Longworth, J., & Arcelus, J. (2017). Prevalence of anxiety symptoms and disorders in the transgender population: A systematic review of the literature. *International Journal of Transgenderism, 18*(1), 27–38. https://doi.org/10.1080/15532739.2016.1258353

9. Witcomb, G. L., Bouman, W. P., Claes, L., Brewin, N., Crawford, J. R., & Arcelus, J. (2018). Levels of depression in transgender people and its predictors: Results of a large matched control study with transgender people accessing clinical services. *Journal of affective disorders, 235,* 308–315. https://doi.org/10.1016/j.jad.2018.02.051

10. Breines, J. G., & Chen, S. (2012). Self-compassion increases self-improvement motivation. *Personality and Social Psychology Bulletin*, *38*(9), 1133–1143. https://doi.org/10.1177/0146167212445599

11. Winders, S. J., Murphy, O., Looney, K., & O'Reilly, G. (2020). Self-compassion, trauma, and posttraumatic stress disorder: A systematic review. *Clinical psychology & psychotherapy, 27*(3), 300–329. https://doi.org/10.1002/cpp.2429

12. Hope, N., Koestner, R., & Milyavskaya, M. (2014). The role of self-compassion in goal pursuit and well-being among university freshmen. *Self and Identity, 13,* 579–593. https://doi.org/10.1080/15298868.2014.889032

13. Hollis-Walker, L., & Colosimo, K. (2011). Mindfulness, self-compassion, and happiness in non- meditators: A theoretical and empirical examination. *Personality and Individual Differences, 50,* 222–227. https://doi.org/10.1016/j.paid.2010.09.033

14. Doorley, J. D., Kashdan, T. B., Weppner, C. H., & Glass, C. R. (2022). The effects of self-compassion on daily emotion regulation and performance rebound among college athletes: Comparisons with confidence, grit, and hope. *Psychology of Sport and Exercise, 58,* 102081. https://doi.org/10.1016/j.psychsport.2021.102081

15. Hughes, M., Brown, S. L., Campbell, S., Dandy, S., & Cherry, M. G. (2021). Self- compassion and anxiety and depression in chronic physical illness populations: A systematic review. *Mindfulness, 12*(7), 1597– 1610. https://doi.org/10.1007/s12671-021-01602-y

16. Raes, F. (2010). Rumination and worry as mediators of the relationship between self- compassion and depression and anxiety. *Personality and Individual Differences, 48*(6), 757–761. https://doi.org/10.1016/j.paid.2010.01.023

17. Suh, H., & Jeong, J. (2021). Association of self-compassion with suicidal thoughts and behaviors and non-suicidal self injury: A

meta-analysis. *Frontiers in Psychology, 12,* 633482. https://doi. org/10.3389/fpsyg.2021.633482

18. Hiçdurmaz, D., & Aydin, A. (2017). The relationship between self-compassion and multidimensional perfectionism levels and influencing factors in nursing students. *Journal of Psychiatric Nursing, 8,* 86–94. https://doi.org/10.14744/phd.2017.40469

Chapter 12

1. Neff, K. D. (2003). Self-compassion: An alternative conceptualization of a healthy attitude toward oneself. *Self and Identity, 2,* 85–102. https://doi.org/10.1080/15298860309032
2. Neff, K. D. & Germer, C. K (2018). *The Mindful self-compassion workbook: A proven way to accept yourself, find inner strength, and thrive.* The Guilford Press.
3. Burnett, M., Newbill, C., Gurin, P. (Executive Producers). (2009-present). *Shark tank* [TV series]. Sony Pictures Television, Inc.

Chapter 13

1. Bowlby, J. (1988). *A secure base: Parent-child attachment and healthy human development.* Basic Books.
2. Bowlby, J. (1983). *Attachment and loss. Vol. 1: Attachment.* Basic Books.
3. Settle, K. (2017). This is me. [Song]. On *The greatest showman: Original motion picture soundtrack* [Album]. Atlantic Records.
4. UMass Boston. (2010, March 12). *Developmental sciences at UMass Boston.* [Video]. Youtube. https://www.youtube.com/ watch?v=vmE3NfB_HhE

Chapter 14

1. Mason, H., Vandoni, M., Debarbieri, G., Codrons, E., Ugargol, V., & Bernardi, L. (2013). Cardiovascular and respiratory effect of yogic slow breathing in the yoga beginner: What is the best approach? *Evidence-Based Complementary and Alternative Medicine, 2013.* https://doi.org/10.1155/2013/743504

2. Vierra, J., Boonla, O., & Prasertsri, P. (2022). Effects of sleep deprivation and 4-7-8 breathing control on heart rate variability, blood pressure, blood glucose, and endothelial function in healthy young adults. *Physiological Reports, 10*(13). https://doi.org/10.14814/phy2.15389

3. Bach, D., Groesbeck, G., Stapleton, P., Sims, R., Blickheuser, K., & Church, D. (2019). Clinical EFT (Emotional Freedom Techniques) improves multiple physiological markers of health. *Journal of Evidence-Based Integrative Medicine, 24.* https://doi.org/10.1177/2515690X18823691

Chapter 15

1. Peterson, C., and Seligman, M. E. P. (2004). *Character strengths and virtues: A handbook and classification.*, American Psychological Association. Oxford University Press.

2. VIA Institute on Character. (n.d). *The VIA Character Strengths Survey.* https://www.viacharacter.org/account/register

3. Azañedo, C. M., Artola, T., Sastre, S., & Alvarado, J. M. (2021). Character strengths predict subjective well-being, psychological well-being, and psychopathological symptoms, over and above functional social support. *Frontiers in Psychology, 12,* 661278. https://doi.org/10.3389/fpsyg.2021.661278

4. Thomas, K. J., da Cunha, J., & Santo, J. B. (2022). Changes in character virtues are driven by classroom relationships: A longitudinal study of elementary school children. *School Mental Health: A Multidisciplinary Research and Practice Journal, 14,* 266–277. https://doi.org/10.1007/s12310-022-09511-8

5. Gradito Dubord, M.-A., Forest, J., Balčiūnaitė, L. M., Rauen, E., & Jungert, T. (2022). The power of strength-oriented feedback enlightened by self-determination theory: A positive technology-based intervention. *Journal of Happiness Studies: An Interdisciplinary Forum on Subjective Well-Being, 23,* 2827– 2848. https://doi.org/10.1007/s10902-022-00524-3

6. Mubashar, T., & Harzer, C. (2023). It takes two to tango: Linking signature strengths use and organizational support for strengths use with organizational outcomes. *Journal of Occupational and Organizational Psychology, 96*(4), 897– 918. https://doi.org/10.1111/joop.12455

7. Bachik, M. A. K., Carey, G., & Craighead, W. E. (2021) Via character strengths among U.S. college students and their associations with happiness, well-being, resiliency, academic success and psychopathology. *Journal of Positive Psychology, 16*(4), 512–525. https://doi.org/10.1080/17439760.2020.1752785

8. Niemiec, R. (2019, June 26). *Tips for using each character strength in a new way.* VIA Institute on Character. https://www.viacharacter.org/topics/articles/tips-for- using-each-character-strength-in-a-new-way

9. Iodice, J. A., Malouff, J. M., & Schutte, N. S. (2021). The association between gratitude and depression: A meta-analysis. *International Journal of Depression and Anxiety, 4*:024. https://doi.org/10.23937/2643-4059/1710024

10. Lin, C. C. (2017). The effect of higher-order gratitude on mental well-being: Beyond personality and unifactoral gratitude. *Current*

Psychology: A Journal for Diverse Perspectives on Diverse Psychological Issues, 36(1), 127– 135. https://doi.org/10.1007/s12144-015-9392-0

11. Witvliet, C. V., Richie, F. J., Luna, L. M. R., & Tongeren, D. R. V. (2019). Gratitude predicts hope and happiness: A two-study assessment of traits and states. *The Journal of Positive Psychology, 14*(3), 271- 282, https://doi.org/10.1080/17439760.2018.1424924

12. Emmons, R. A., & McCullough, M. E. (2003). Counting blessings versus burdens: an experimental investigation of gratitude and subjective well-being in daily life. *Journal of personality and social psychology, 84*(2), 377–389. https://doi.org/10.1037//0022-3514.84.2.377

13. Toepfer, S. M. (2019). Letters of gratitude as a methos for improving family relationship quality. *International Review of Modern Sociology, 45*(2), 125–140. https://www.jstor.org/stable/48602760

14. Lyubomirsky, S. (2007). *The how of happiness.* The Penguin Press HC.

Chapter 16

1. Stanton, A., Unkrich, L. (Directors). (2003). *Finding Nemo* [Film]. Pixar Animation Studios.

About the Author

Z. Seda Şahin, Ph.D., LMFT is a psychotherapist, an AAMFT Clinical Fellow, and an Approved Supervisor. She earned her doctorate from Purdue University and previously served as an associate professor and clinic director. Over the past twenty years, Dr. Seda has provided therapy, coaching, and consulting services to individuals, couples, families, and groups.

www.ingramcontent.com/pod-product-compliance
Lightning Source LLC
Chambersburg PA
CBHW070657130626
46553CB00005B/1735